MW01094319

COSMIC COMMAND

by

VERNON HOWARD

NEW LIFE FOUNDATION
Pine, Arizona 85544

Second Printing 1994
Copyright 1979 by Vernon Howard

ISBN 0-911203-24-9

FOR INFORMATION ON CLASSES, BOOKS,
TAPES AND VIDEO CASSETTES, WRITE:
NEW LIFE
PO BOX 2230
PINE, ARIZONA 85544

SIX WAYS TO USE THIS BOOK

Read this book as if it can change your entire life. It can.

You now hold in your hands a complete library of the great wisdoms of the ages. Practical knowledge is presented in clear and simple language, saving you years of search and study. Ready for instant use, it will give you now what you want right now.

Some of the truths may surprise you at first, may even seem strange. This is the perfectly normal and usual experience of everyone, and is simply the first right step up the side of the mountain. In time you will see all these facts as kindly and helpful friends whose only purpose is to guide you to the heights of a free life.

A special term has been created for this book: Cosmic Command. You will meet it at various places. The higher principles in this book make Cosmic Command your own new and permanent power, capable of conquering every daily event.

1. You can start reading this book at any place you like. Go down the *Guide to Topics* and select any subject that attracts your interest or that offers help in a present condition. While reading the ideas try to connect them with the problem you wish to solve.

2. Ponder a sentence deeply. Review, reflect, search out its higher meanings which are surely there. Each sentence is like the branch of a fruitful peach tree. The abundant harvest is yours for the taking.

3. As you read, write down the numbers of the sentences which make a deep impression upon your mind. The impression means that the higher ideas in print are contacting your own higher parts. It is like the happy meeting of two princes of the cosmic kingdom. Review these impressive ideas often.

4. Carry this book with you whenever possible. Make the most of spare moments by reading a page or two. Your class can be wherever you are. Many of the sentences in this book were presented for the first time in the author's own classes and lectures.

5. You may wish to join or start a class to study these wisdoms. Sincere students in a large or small group can be of great help to each other. Several sections in this book offer aid in conducting classes.

6. Remember always that these truths are on your side, in your favor, regardless of how it may appear at times. Every idea will finally become clear and helpful as you earnestly climb up toward Cosmic Command. So proceed as if a new and victorious life is just ahead of you, for it is.

Vernon Howard

GUIDE TO TOPICS

COSMIC COMMAND

FIRST PRINCIPLES OF COSMIC COMMAND

1. Cosmic Command is simply a right part of anyone, the conscious part, the kingdom of heaven within.

2. Cosmic Command does not consist of craving or imagination or of ordinary thinking, but of God, supreme truth.

3. Many times during your day, suddenly ask yourself, "What is carrying me away from Cosmic Command?"

4. When noticing how you are carried away by a worry or daydream or whatever, call yourself back to yourself at once.

5. Cosmic Command is eternal.

6. Cosmic Command is victorious over everything, including any troubles which you think are much too much for you.

EASY FIRST STEPS

7. Wish to start inner enrichment and you have started.

8. All you need to know to start the inner path is to know the emptiness of your present life.

9. Everyone starts with desperation, but the wise seeker turns his desperation toward insight, not bitterness.

10. The very entering of the dark tunnel is the first light in ending its darkness.

11. Understanding can begin by understanding that your present solutions solve nothing.

12. Each time you think you want to change something, think about changing yourself.

13. Only when fully convinced we have been living the wrong way are we ready to learn the right way.

14. Curiously, self-rescue can start by awareness of our very unwillingness to seek higher facts.

15. Build your refusal to accept answers from yourself or others which you sense are wrong.

16. Develop discernment.

17. It is a thousand times more sensible to climb one foot up the mountainside than to chatter for years about the mountaintop.

18. Just begin at the beginning, which is to know that you need to know.

WISE GUIDES FOR SWIFT SUCCESS

19. There exists a great wisdom surpassing ordinary human knowledge, and you are now reading about it.

20. Groping in the dark at first is a perfectly normal and right way to feel your way toward the light.

21. The usual kind of life on earth *is* futile, but only because we have not as yet found our cosmic purpose.

22. You qualify as a student in the cosmic college if you no longer know what to believe.

2

23. With this new knowledge you communicate healthy messages to yourself.

24. Whatever has been lost can now be found, including the lost man or woman.

25. The only sensible thing to do with the human trap is to get out of it.

26. Ponder day and night the idea that human beings are now inwardly asleep, but can awaken with true knowledge.

27. These studies are perfect for anyone who feels the emptiness of his life.

28. It is a perfectly good attitude to earnestly seek truth just to see what happens.

29. The life unfolds from what we *think* is true, so what is more important to the life than to examine our thinking?

30. True forgiveness for every badness begins the moment one attempts to understand himself and his life.

31. There is no risk at all in deciding that real happiness resides in inner trueness, not in outer riches.

32. A right search starts by realizing that you do not know what you are searching for.

33. Only a very small part of a person wants the truth at first, but that small part is a great start.

34. Meeting these higher messages is the most important event in anyone's life.

THE TRULY PRACTICAL LIFE

35. When acted upon, these principles make a man or woman of practical use to himself or herself.

36. Work on facts and they will eventually work on you.

37. People who say that spiritual truths are impractical for earthly affairs are merely evading their inner dishonesty.

38. Learn to recognize a negative social atmosphere when seeing it, and remember it need not invade you.

39. These ideas are truly scientific, for they probe into the real cause of human problems, then reveal the cure.

40. You can read your own inner powers just as plainly as you are now reading the words in this book.

41. Self-wholeness alone is practical.

42. A man can live rightly from himself or he can live wrongly from thousands of wrong instructions from thousands of wrong people.

43. The difficulties of waking up are nothing compared to the difficulties of remaining asleep.

44. Seek cosmic comprehension, for whatever is within your comprehension is also within your power.

CONFUSION CAN BE ENDED

45. If you do not know what to do with your life, you need only unite with truth, for it knows exactly what you really need to do, and will tell you.

4

46. Instead of wondering what to do, realize you can find out.

47. Confusion need not stop your progress any more than darkness can stop a sailing ship.

48. Your own mind can either clarify or confuse your own mind.

49. Fearing confusion is as unnecessary as fearing angry butterflies.

50. Delusion is confusion.

51. A confused mind trying to understand society's confusion is like a sparrow trying to understand a hurricane.

52. Why guess at life when it can be known?

53. Facts are the forces which clear away confusion, but we must prefer the facts over our confusions.

54. Living without self-insight is like driving a car at night without lights.

55. Never be persuaded that chaos is ever right, or that it can ever create orderliness.

56. Do not take confusion toward these ideas as an enemy to be battled, but simply as an area to pass through.

HOW TO UNDERSTAND HIGHER TRUTHS

57. Read higher truths with a light and adventurous spirit that wants at all costs to discover what is truly true.

58. Be aware of your own resistance to higher facts, for that very awareness dissolves resistance.

59. Realize that higher truths do not make sense at first to anyone still under the spell of spiritual sleep, for he does not know he is asleep.

60. Understanding occurs when an outer truth is met by an inner willingness.

61. The only way to do something truly important every day is to seek to understand yourself every day.

62. Untruth lies and tells you that higher truths will hurt you, but it is untruth itself that injures.

63. Truth never wishes to frighten, but wishes only to awaken.

64. Mere intellect cannot comprehend higher truths, but you can rise to your eternal nature which comprehends perfectly.

THE TWO SEXES

65. A foolish man meets a gullible woman and they foolishly and gullibly agree to call it love.

66. No one should ever use the word *love* without wondering whether he really knows its meaning.

67. Mental freedom from another person cancels the pain of not getting what you want from him or her.

68. Losing someone will be as falsely painful as it was falsely joyous when meeting him.

69. Sex is under command when it can be thought about without arousing any kind of nervousness.

70. Your wrong desire toward another person is a signal to him or her to take advantage of you.

71. A man or a woman with a harmful motive toward you will never look at it, but you should.

72. Maybe you really do not want that other person after all, but want freedom from wanting him.

73. Two imaginary people meet, imagining they are real, causing grief.

74. When two deluded human beings meet to discuss love and cooperation, truth has no part in that discussion.

75. When someone is sexually right, he or she can take it or leave it without conflict.

76. There must be no hostility toward a treacherous man or woman, and with real insight there will be none.

77. Both he and she are afraid to find the other out.

78. Detect artificial love, which is easily done by noticing how hateful it can be when thwarted.

79. Love exists where there is no hopeful waiting for something from the other person.

80. The only person who can really be concerned with you is someone who has risen above his own self-concern.

ENJOY YOURSELF

81. Find your real self and you automatically find real enjoyment.

82. Anyone who cannot rightly enjoy his own company cannot rightly enjoy the company of others.

83. It can be just as nice a day inside you as outside.

84. People and objects are rightly enjoyed when the false self is not attached to them.

85. The search for truth is really a lot of good fun.

86. Right thinking increases our capacity for enjoying ourselves in the physical and social world.

87. Discover what it really means to enjoy yourself, and you will.

88. Life is finally enjoyed when we understand clearly what it means to live without unnecessary thoughts, emotions, actions, speech, involvements.

DO NOT BE GULLIBLE

89. Gullibility cannot see itself as gullibility, but Cosmic Command can be called in to point it out.

90. Exploitation by others starts with self-exploitation, that is, we damage ourselves because of refusals to look and learn.

91. Gullibility connects closely with a wrong use of the power of imagination.

92. Quiet ignorance in human authorities is often mistaken for poised wisdom.

93. Gullibility calls itself many flattering names, including faith, trust, devotion, loyalty and love.

94. Delusion can appear very attractive.

95. Every sleeping person is exploited in ways which would horrify him if he were to see them suddenly and fully.

96. An unconscious wish to exploit others will block awareness of exploitation by others.

97. Gullibility is based in unawareness of personal evil, which makes one an unaware victim of the evil in others.

98. People interested in getting something from you are experts in showing interest in you.

99. You may be sorry if you become involved with people who try to make you feel sorry for them.

100. A truly strong individual cannot be exploited by others.

101. If shocked or hurt by bad human behavior we are gullible, preferring fantasies about people over facts.

102. Exploited people are reluctant to look at their exploitation, but it is a healthy necessity for the cure.

RECEIVE THESE LESSONS

103. Once we know a spiritual fact we must not linger with it but must proceed until living it.

104. We live a spiritual fact to the extent that we have detected and dropped vanity and pretense.

105. One talent supplied by higher wisdom is the talent for remaining silent while others chatter compulsively.

106. Each person must live with himself.

107. A friend-in-truth is one who does not expect you to behave better than your present consciousness allows.

108. What you really want is the disappearance of directionless days.

109. Almost everyone who says he is awakened is not.

110. A man's degree of delusion will be equaled by his angry denial of it.

111. Society will not tolerate the calling of human madness by its right name.

112. Nothing, absolutely nothing, is really on your side except the truth which exists above your own beliefs.

RIGHT REBELLION

113. Right rebellion starts by seeing that we have taken our artificial and harmful nature as being true and good.

114. Breaking the wrong rules of the usual nature is essential if we are to live with the liberations of the new nature.

115. It is right and necessary to rebel against the boring routines of life, but with the guidance of higher knowledge.

116. There is a right kind of rebellion in which you rebel against being afraid of *anything*.

117. Rebel rightly by remembering that hostile feelings live in you at your expense.

118. Remember, you must rebel against your own misunderstanding, and not against exterior people and conditions.

FREE YOURSELF FROM FALSE DUTIES

119. A first step in freedom from false duties is to learn to recognize one when it tries to take you over.

120. A false duty arises from a divided nature, and will therefore contain strain and confusion and many doubts.

121. Self-unawareness drags us into false and resented duties.

122. You are not required to save the world, but only yourself, which is the same as saving the world.

123. We need to erase heavy imaginations about what we need.

124. A self-image interferes with spontaneous action, as when unable to relax because of the nagging of an imaginary duty.

125. It is not your duty to try to make someone understand who does not want to understand.

126. You are not required to do anything for others which is harmful to you.

127. If the human involvement or the social duty is burdensome, it is artificial, and should be dropped.

128. Decency is a natural expression of your natural self, and therefore can never be a burdensome duty.

129. It is unnecessary to anxiously give your mind something to think about.

130. You are never required to be recognized as important by either other people or yourself.

131. Do not allow lazy people to burden you with their own responsibilities, which they will try to do by calling for your "cooperation" or "compassion" or "social contribution."

132. Anyone burdened with his own illusions will feel compelled to burden you with them.

133. A false spiritual life consisting of parroted religious phrases and obedience to man-made doctrines is a dreadful burden.

134. There are many things we do not need to know, such as ways for impressing other people.

135. You are not required to please anyone who hints or demands that you please him.

136. You are here on earth to find yourself, not prove yourself.

ESSENTIAL KNOWLEDGE

137. Egotism is exceedingly cunning in masquerading as goodness, generosity, spirituality and as nonegotism.

138. Only unconscious egotists are deceived and injured by cunning egotists.

139. If a fox values rubies, the ego values rightness.

140. Failure to understand life is caused largely by the ego's wish to not understand.

141. Cosmic Command is growing when we see we are not really thrilled by what we think thrills us.

142. Simply be deeply interested in your own enlightenment.

143. What a strange working of the laws of chance that it is *always* the other person's fault!

144. Only a clear mind can appreciate clear thinking when observing it.

145. You need not follow the painful demands which insist you must follow them, such as the demand to please others.

146. Honest self-observation reveals that you are different than imagined, which is great news.

INNER SLEEP AND SELF-AWAKENING

147. Regardless of exterior appearances, the vast majority of human beings dwell in a state of inner sleep.

148. Every sleeping person is convinced he is awake.

149. Ten thousand questions are answered by the advice, "Learn what it means to awaken from spiritual sleep."

150. An unawakened mind is like a sailboat pushed around by changeable winds.

151. Every contact with people can be used in one way or another for self-awakening.

152. Awakening from inner sleep is hastened by various jolts of seeing how asleep we are.

153. Sleeping people have a strict rule by which they agree to call each other awakened people.

154. Sensibleness shortens psychic sleep.

155. Asking a sleeping man to not be angry is like asking a storm to not be furious.

156. We are asleep if we cling to religious ideas, but still feel lost and worried and isolated.

157. People dimly sense they are asleep, which is why they feel a strange shock when advised, "Wake up!"

158. Like awakening in the hills at dawn, self-awakening explains surrounding realities.

ALL ABOUT SELF-DIVIDED PEOPLE

159. Most human beings are so busy doing nothing, which they call something, they are unable to see how they could truly do something.

160. Badness is pained by the existence of goodness.

161. Personal enemies are created only when the mind wrongly believes in a separate self.

162. Silence terrifies loud psychic sickness.

163. People detect fear as weakness, which it is, and will wrongly try to take advantage of it.

164. The unteachable are the most sure that they can teach.

165. Those who feel they are victims will be most eager to make victims of others.

166. Life is treacherous only to unawakened minds, for treachery conceals itself only in unawakened minds.

167. Stupidity is bored with true intelligence.

168. The worst thing about the advice of self-deluded people is that they have to follow it.

169. Desperation cannot hear instruction.

170. In this peculiar world a man who has no idea of what he really wants can always tell other people just what they want.

171. Self-ignorance and self-injury are brothers.

172. The last thing anyone wants to see is that he is the cause of his own grief, for that would destroy his conceited illusion that he knows what he is doing with his life.

173. People often use fancy words to warn you against people who use fancy words.

174. Public reformers live in private despair.

175. You understand human nature when you are never surprised by anything it does.

176. Human beings love agitation, which is like loving a tornado.

177. To make today's anguish repeat itself tomorrow, a man need only remain the kind of a person he is today.

178. Let these facts about people prove them-selves, for example, observe how conceit and hostility go together.

YOU NEED NOT FEEL HELPLESS

179. You are not kicked around by real life, but only by false life which you imagine is real.

180. Self-centered imagination breeds dis-appointment.

181. Let the growth of despair be matched by your effort to see through its bluff.

182. Moment by moment awareness of what you are doing guarantees control of each moment.

183. Our seeking may start with desperation, but finding is the result of abandoning desperation.

184. Do not ask how to drop desperation, but simply drop it.

185. If feeling that life is going on without you, see it as a false feeling arising from the false self.

186. Do not be ashamed of anxiously seeking help, but be aware that you are doing so.

187. Darkness is destroyed by daring it to do its worst to you.

188. The frustrated or depressed self may exist as a temporary experience, but does not exist as a permanent necessity.

WELCOME HEALTHY INFLUENCES

189. To not suffer from wrong influences, place yourself under your own right influences.

190. Anyone who tries to distort a bit of truth you have found is trying to damage you.

191. It is a world of skilled actors and actresses who will try to influence you for their own benefit.

192. A person who has no mind of his own will fiercely try to prevent others from having minds of their own.

193. Remember, the world is filled with people who do not know who they are, who spend their lives telling other people who they are.

194. The healthy influence of Cosmic Command reaches those who gladly place themselves under it.

AUTHENTIC SAFETY AND SECURITY

195. Perhaps one man in a million really sees the danger of self-ignorance.

196. Knowledge of Cosmic Command is the only real and enduring protection.

197. In this curious world, people run to danger for safety, like a sheep seeking help from a wolf.

198. Trust absolutely who you really are, but never trust who you are not.

199. We fall into our self-made pits.

200. It is hazardous imagination to see goodness in oneself or in others where it does not in fact exist.

201. Human stupidity is dangerous only to stupid humans.

202. Studying one's own confusion is not a risky action, to the contrary, it begins to remove risks in life.

203. End hazardous thoughts and you end hazardous involvements.

204. Insight is protection against deception, like glimpsing a trap on a jungle trail.

205. Have no part of the world of savage smilers.

206. To stop taking society's nonsense seriously we must first rise above our own nonsense we take as serious.

207. When admitting we are wrong we reduce the haunting insecurity of living wrongly.

208. Truth is the only castle of safety for the frightened fugitive.

209. Ask truth to teach you, not take care of you, for its teachings will take care of you.

OBTAIN TRUE GUIDANCE

210. Let your real nature be your only authority.

211. You will never go wrong by asking your real self what it knows.

212. Choose the truly right and you can ignore the result, for it will be truly right for you.

213. Your happy goal is to finally give your own daily guidance to your own daily steps.

214. Follow facts.

215. Learn to give yourself new and higher advice.

216. Only those capable of recognizing a source of true wisdom can draw from it.

217. Obey natural essence, not acquired opinions.

218. Cosmic inspiration is released by getting ourselves out of our own way.

219. Learn it today and it will guide you tomorrow.

THE WONDERS OF INNER TRANSFORMATION

220. You cannot understand life by itself, but you can understand yourself, which includes a comprehension of life.

221. If someone is at war with you, but you are not at war with him, you will not suffer war wounds.

222. These teachings reveal stars you never before knew existed in the spiritual skies.

223. You are free when you do not know what to do with yourself and it does not make you nervous.

224. No one can know how high another man has climbed up the mountain until he reaches the same lofty level himself.

225. Something other than you can and will rescue you.

226. When you finally love truth more than you love another person, you truly love that person for the first time.

227. Something magnificent happens when one small part of you submits to rightness at the same time that your other ninety-nine parts rage in hostility against the submission.

228. The feeling of doing what is right will finally conquer the demanding false pleasure of doing what is wrong.

229. "Remember and obey cosmic principles" is the majestic method which changes everything in your life.

230. Remain in your own right inner place and there cannot be a wrong outer place for you, though it may be wrong for others.

231. The past casts no shadows on anyone in cosmic light.

232. We appreciate something other than the self when perceiving something other than the self.

233. You are lifted into the conscious by the observance of and detachment from the mechanical, as when impartially watching irritation instead of unconsciously enjoying it.

234. A chief feature of inner illness is to be tensely on guard, while a chief feature of inner health is to be casually alert.

235. When you learn the lesson in the pain you will not have to repeat either the lesson or the pain.

BE AT EASE

236. Instead of trying to force life to conform to you, let life teach you that forcing is unnecessary.

237. Study naturalness, for naturalness is authentic ease.

238. It is an interesting fact that a real life is both highly active and yet always leisurely.

239. Let life happen, but not according to demands.

240. Correct the mind and we lose the burden of trying to correct everything else.

241. A knowing mind rests.

242. Once gained, a true idea maintains itself effortlessly in the mind, like a well-loved king.

243. Cosmic Command handles exterior changes easily.

TWENTY PROFOUND PRINCIPLES

244. When not knowing what to do with yourself, just be aware there is no need to wonder what to do, for essence knows.

245. High or low, the quality of the pursued will match the quality of the pursuer.

246. Your future is determined by your nature.

247. A man always does something for the real reason he does it, for at that moment he can only do what he really is.

248. The abandonment of wrong thoughts is hard at first because all our false ideas about ourselves are invested in them.

249. Real rescue is beyond whatever you can now think about, for real rescue is the new.

250. When you no longer look for a way out of suffering you will no longer suffer.

251. You can accept anything that comes naturally of itself, but when that happens there is no longer a question of accepting or rejecting.

252. Fear is incapable of loving anything higher than itself.

253. There is no person *and* his life, for the person's very nature makes up all the life he has.

254. A person who commands himself rightly will command others rightly, which is a rare spiritual manifestation.

255. What a man calls his success and his failure is simply the opposite sides of his self-centered imagination.

256. Only a spiritual genius can react without vanity when having power to grant or deny an urgent request.

257. Lose yourself and you will find yourself.

258. Anyone who can be shown that he is really not interested in certain activities is one who can find himself.

259. All we need to overcome is the wrong thought that there is something we need to overcome.

260. Only silence has good hearing.

261. You will be able to do what you really want to do when you are no longer compelled to do what you now do.

262. A new and healthy experience will occur if you will not take sides with your own opinions!

263. Finally, the inward battle between *yes* and *no* comes to an end, and the suppressed scream is heard no more.

INSIGHT INTO CONTROL

264. An egotistical man imagines he controls his own destiny, refusing to see himself as the helpless puppet he is.

265. Imagination imagines it can and does control things, but imaginary control is no control at all.

266. Demanding personal domination over outer events is a sign of absence of inner control.

267. Control means to not be carried away from oneself by unexpected events or by one's own rising thoughts.

268. Self-control does not consist of suppressing fiery feelings but to not have them at all.

269. Just as a donkey has no interest in books, imaginary control is not interested in studying real control.

270. The larger the crowd the less individual control, as seen in the reckless violence of mad mobs.

271. The study of cosmic consciousness is of supreme importance, for consciousness *is* control.

272. Real control can start by studying the difference between mechanical and conscious behavior.

273. Cosmic Command alone is capable of controlling one's life rightly.

DEVELOP COSMIC ENERGY

274. Positive energy is that which arises from man's profound nature to direct every activity.

275. Weakness is simply lack of self-knowledge and life-knowledge, so now we know how to become strong.

276. Like riding a strong but nervous horse, keep tugging your energy back onto the path to higher understanding.

277. There is fresh power in simply realizing that we do not as yet understand something.

278. Weakness has no real power over us, but appears to have because we are temporarily apart from Cosmic Command.

279. Develop even a bit of natural energy and it will connect you with all the energy in the universe.

ABSORB THESE IDEAS

280. The first thing a man must be told is the last thing he wants to hear, which is, "There is something wrong with you."

281. A major error of many teachings is believing that most men and women would welcome offered truth.

282. Truth is a place you can always go to with full acceptance.

283. New students often make a curious mistake with a teacher—trying to teach him what it is all about!

284. People who would not tolerate political tyranny submit meekly to the dictatorship of their own negative natures.

285. Ignorance outwits the ignorant person every time.

286. A beginner is not asked to be real, for he cannot be, but he is asked to observe his unreality, which can be done.

287. The more a man treats others with contempt, the more he demands that others treat him with respect.

288. Control of reactions is control of life.

289. One purpose in reading this book is to allow book knowledge to become your personal insight.

HAVE RIGHT HUMAN RELATIONS

290. When really knowing yourself you also know how to relate rightly to people and events.

291. Let the right part of you handle the wrong part of another person and you will come out right.

292. It is not your duty to make another person happy, nor is it in your power to do so.

293. It is not another person's duty to make you happy, nor is it in his power to do so.

294. Everyone is handled competently by realizing that no one can behave better than his present level of life-comprehension.

295. We are wrongly connected with other people only by our own wrong thoughts.

296. Live up to your own rightness, not to what other people expect of you.

297. Speak of the possibilities of goodness in people only *after* speaking of their present badness.

298. When with any human being, just remember there is much more boiling inside him than you can imagine.

299. Stay as far away as possible from those who glorify their persecution—the persecution they invite.

300. It is real liking when you like what is real in another person because it is the same reality you like in yourself.

301. We can let another person be himself only when we want nothing from him.

302. Never enter a human relationship in which unhealthy attitudes dominate the atmosphere.

303. Do not give your life away to the neurosis of other people, for it is not required of you.

304. The point is not whether you are accepted or rejected by others, but whether you are freeing yourself of both slaveries.

305. Knowing its own true value, your real self is above both acceptance and rejection by others.

LAWS OF ATTRACTION

306. You attract the right way only when you have exhausted and been exhausted by the wrong way.

307. Right attracts right, and wrong attracts wrong.

308. An absolute requirement for attracting higher goodness is to courageously see through self-deception.

309. For good or bad, we attract what we *assume* is sensible.

310. A negative nature attracts negative experiences, while a free nature is its own free experiences.

311. We attract the same things that we send out.

312. Realize that inner disorder can never be good for you, for that realization can attract inner orderliness.

313. To attract something higher, *be* someone higher.

THE ARTIFICIAL SELF

314. The artificial self is made up of self-centered thinking, negative feelings and unconscious actions.

315. The false self thinks self-change is scary and impossible, but the real nature knows better.

316. Remember that anything really instructive to our true nature will not be welcomed by our artificial self.

317. The counterfeit self calls anything evil that does not support or praise its artificiality.

318. Taking surface personality as real is as wrong as taking the shadow of a man as the man himself.

319. Feeling persecuted by a cruel fate is just another trick of the false self to keep itself the center of attention.

320. Nothing makes the life harder than unseen artificiality.

321. We give up the invented personality when seeing that it is good, not bad, for us to do so.

322. The surface self becomes nervous when finding itself outside its familiar prison grounds.

323. Rigid wrongness is like a broken clock without inner life which must always say the same thing.

324. The artificial self has the weird talent to dream it is behaving kindly, even while destroying everything it meets.

325. As we begin to see that we live with an unconscious artificial identity we begin to understand everything else.

DARING AND BOLDNESS

326. Have no timidity in discovering that life is different than you always believed.

327. Real knowledge supplies right boldness.

328. A small boat hugs the shore, while a large boat explores broad seas and finds treasure islands.

329. Boldly close the door of the past behind you.

330. The daring applauded by angels is to start daring to not be who you have always been.

331. We must cancel our refusal to search beyond our usual ways.

332. To know more, dare more.

333. One kind of healthy daring is to dare to let someone valuable to you lose interest in you.

334. For your own sake, go through what you must go through.

335. True bravery consists largely of going against your own negative momentum.

336. If it is necessary to get your feet wet while crossing the river, get them wet, but cross.

337. Spiritual daring is to dare the loss of and to actually lose stubborn opinions in oneself.

338. Take the bold initiative in your own deliverance.

339. One way to learn who you really are is to risk the displeasure of everyone who wants you to remain in the dark.

340. The inner battle cannot be won by running away from it.

341. It is both brave and intelligent to destroy the ideas which have made our lives what they now are.

342. Boldly inform your own feelings of dread that you will no longer tolerate them.

343. Venture valorously.

CONSTRUCTIVE THOUGHTS

344. Know that the right path reveals sudden surprises, strange sights, unique explanations, fresh inspirations.

345. Sensing that we are our own frustration is not enough, for the cure resides in acting rightly toward it.

346. Truthful attitudes alone are positive attitudes.

347. There is an alternative to man-made wrongness, but it is not man-made rightness.

348. Man-made rightness is wrong, as when showing exterior kindness in order to get something from others.

349. When defending himself a man is simply defending his acquired ideas about himself, which is not at all his true self.

350. Higher insight alone knows when to say yes and when to say no.

351. A weak person who wants others to be strong for him will be unable to recognize a truly strong person when meeting one.

352. Never avoid any kind of difficulty, for Cosmic Command knows exactly what to do about it.

353. It is a good sign that you have read this book up to this point.

A FRIENDLY INVITATION

354. Truth urges, "Perplexed humans, come to your senses."

355. We are not accused of being permanently bad, but are invited to see and be something else.

356. When truth can do something with us, it can do something for us.

357. Truth is like a flag on top of a castle, signaling a friendly invitation to right companionship.

358. We are invited to solve our problems by outgrowing them.

359. Truth invites our return, anytime, but on its terms, not ours.

THE BEAUTY OF SELF-WHOLENESS

360. The only reason anyone needs for becoming whole is that it is better than being split.

361. Wholeness can see how everything connects, such as one's natural connection with everyone else.

362. Instructing memory alone causes life-limitation, while instructing the whole person invites an unlimited life.

363. Only the niceness of self-wholeness can behave rightly toward unnice people.

364. Feeling pleasure in disorder goes against self-wholeness.

365. A whole person does not make promises later regretted, which is reason enough to attain self-wholeness.

366. Few human beings see the difference between mechanical religion and living with inner wholeness.

367. Surface religion speaks from memory goaded by vanity, while true religion speaks from wholeness.

368. The pleasures enjoyed by the whole individual are always with him.

369. To advance from ego-interest to wholeness-interest we must see it is the only good and happy course to take.

HOW YOU WILL BE DIFFERENT

370. When you are no longer a part of false human life you will be able to walk in and out of human affairs as you please.

371. Truth can set you free from fear of people who are angry with you.

372. An awakened mind has a special kind of audacity which has no fear of criticism or rejection.

373. When consciousness meets a crisis, the crisis disappears.

374. One day you will see more for yourself than you will be able to explain to others.

375. Let truth lead you where you do not want to go, and in time you will want to go.

376. The words "spiritual sleep" have no meaning to those in sleep, being understood only by the awakened.

377. You will develop a natural sense of self-protection having no fear in it.

378. Wondering how and what to think toward life-situations will one day be a thing of the past.

379. A free man cannot hurt others, nor can others hurt him.

380. When really understanding oneself, there is no fear of being misunderstood by others.

381. Your own natural light will replace society's artificial light, just as sunshine replaces electric light.

WHY THE WORLD SPINS DIZZILY

382. Society's cures for society are like trying to pour medicine out of an empty bottle.

383. Man is so used to substitutes for truth that he mindlessly calls his substitutes the truth.

384. Wars are caused by human beings who deny their inner wars.

385. When one sleeping person meets another sleeping person they both proceed to drag each other down.

386. There is no reality in a reputation.

387. The primary purpose of many human organizations is to invent reasons for their existence.

388. Weakness demands that others call it strength.

389. Those who could lead society rightly are neither recognized nor invited by a society which dislikes rightness.

390. A ridiculous mind sees the sensible as ridiculous.

391. Trying to make the truth popular with human beings is like trying to make sheep value silver.

392. The more a sleeping mind tries to straighten things out the worse they get.

393. Fifty wrong minds thinking together will produce fifty wrong answers.

394. Organized neurosis is never called that.

395. Unconscious participation in social silliness is what perpetuates it.

396. The irresponsible fiercely protect the irresponsible.

397. There is no way to make sense out of human affairs, for there is none, and to see this makes the calm sense you need.

398. Almost all social programs for human betterment consist of interfering self-interest.

399. Society's destruction always proceeds in the name of construction.

400. Human society is composed of little boys and girls who are afraid to grow up.

401. Until human nature changes, nothing else changes.

TRUE INTELLIGENCE

402. True intelligence begins by sensing that we are not living from natural wisdom but from hounding thoughts.

403. Whoever sees that trouble is always wherever he is, is getting wise.

404. You cannot ask a more intelligent question than, "How am I thinking incorrectly?"

405. Error seeks to smother natural intelligence, while truth wishes to uncover it.

406. Trying to understand what it means to work internally on yourself is good internal work on yourself.

407. It is a sign of sense to know we need correction.

408. Your wisdom is growing when you no longer believe people who insist they want to hear the truth about themselves.

409. Only a conscious person judges truly, for he is free of the demanding and distorting artificial self.

410. The presence of authentic intelligence is equal to the absence of ego-defense.

411. Real wisdom resides in the silent space between two thoughts.

CONSCIOUSNESS AND AWARENESS

412. Trying to understand life with ordinary thought is like trying to make a wooden bird fly.

413. Above ordinary thought is cosmic consciousness, awareness of reality, which understands and acts rightly.

414. Recognition of spiritual gold *as* spiritual gold is the same as obtaining it.

415. Unawareness cuts us off from our own true good.

416. One valuable awareness is to see how your words or acts arouse a particular kind of reaction in others.

417. Awareness is truth out of the box.

418. React to a mistake properly, for instance, note that it was caused by acting mechanically instead of consciously.

419. Guilty self-condemnation is wrong, while a simple awareness of being wrong is right.

420. To even see you do not know the right questions to ask is one kind of valuable awareness.

421. Consciousness is true conquest.

422. Be grateful, not resistant, to anything that makes you aware that you were unaware.

423. Be aware of your fear of revenge from people you leave because you can no longer play the deceptive game with them.

424. A conscious mind knows *now*, not after it has thought it over.

425. Become more aware that you do not have the answers, which will increase anxiety at first, but eventually end it.

426. Raise fears into awareness, for example, the fear that a loved one might be able to live without you.

427. Be conscious of what you are doing at the moment you are doing it, and watch how you change inwardly.

PASS THROUGH INNER STORMS

428. When storms fall on anyone it is simply because he has chosen to stand in that particular psychic spot.

429. Fighting stormy thoughts only increases them, while seeking insight into them decreases the storm.

430. Happily, it is possible to use a stormy situation for more insight even while getting battered by it.

431. You learn that it is possible to calm the storm by trying to do it with higher help.

432. We do not dislike another person, rather, we dislike the inner storm we imagine he caused.

433. When entering a new storm, remember the strength added by passing consciously through a past storm.

WIN BY LOSING

434. We win by losing, as when we lose self-centeredness and thus win freedom from self-anxiety.

435. There is really no such thing as winning over another person—there is only the *idea* of winning, which has a high price.

436. Each time you let the other person win the ego-victory, you win a true victory.

437. Losses taken with insight increase insight.

438. We have nothing to lose and a real life to win by absorbing these higher facts.

439. When seeing what must be lost for the sake of truth, lose it as fast as possible, for example, imaginary rightness.

440. Simplicity wins by being simple.

441. If you must lose friends for the sake of rightness, lose them at once and never regret it.

442. If you believe in a self which must win, you must also gloomily believe in a self which must lose.

443. Once won, reality can never be lost.

444. See imaginations about yourself *as* imaginations and you will see what it means to lose your life in order to live.

445. Reality wins simply by being real, just as an eagle dominates the sky by being an eagle.

SEE THROUGH THE GIGANTIC HOAX

446. The next time an inner terror tries to intimidate you, see it as a powerless hoax, *even if you do not feel it as such.*

447. Observe and then ignore mental imps that scream for your attention.

448. No fear is more false than the fear of stepping outside of the customary world and its ways.

449. Mental terror has no power of its own, but must rely upon the misunderstanding of the terrified.

450. An enlightened mind never returns hatred for hatred because it is not hoaxed by hatred's false power.

451. Rightly defy inner tyrants by deliberately doing everything the old nature does not want you to do, such as persisting in inner work.

452. Do not listen when harmful voices tell you all the reasons why you should obey them.

453. The only difference in deceivers is in the ways they try to convince you they are not deceivers.

38

454. Take as a fact that fear is a gigantic hoax, then use all these truths to expose the hoax.

455. March right into an obstacle which seems solid, and after passing through you will see it was made of paper.

456. Release the part of you that wants to break out, and it will show you that all obstacles are hoaxes.

457. Cease to obey negative forces in yourself and others, and their tyranny will end.

458. You are not compelled to give fearful attention to haunting thoughts and feelings.

459. Weakness tyrannizes everyone it can hoax.

460. The human conspiracy to keep each other under psychic hypnosis is so overpowering that few ever see though it.

461. A billion sleeping people have no power to stop one small but right part within someone who wants to awaken.

HUMAN EVIL AND BADNESS

462. Trying to stop human badness with moral codes is as effective as scolding an erupting volcano.

463. People are very much against evil, providing that it is the other person's evil.

464. Evil is not really envious of good, for it does not know good, but simply craves to be more evil than the other evil.

465. Truth is attacked in the name of truth.

466. Since evil exists on the mechanical level, it has no choice but to twist everything to serve its dark needs.

467. If you think evil really wins, look at the suppressed nervousness of the winners.

468. Evil acts are rewarded by evil men.

469. Trying to correct human badness without internal correction is like cleaning the outside of a defective car.

470. A demon who tried to imitate an angel could fool other demons but not angels.

471. People trade in evil because of an inability to recognize it as evil for everyone involved.

472. Personal evil hides itself by battling public evil.

473. Most human learning only increases the desire to dominate and destroy.

474. Justifying evil in others arises from justifying evil in oneself, and everyone suffers from it.

475. When hatred gets nervous, any target will do.

476. Evil is mechanical action which does not know it is mechanical and does not want to be told about it.

477. Violence always lies about its motive.

478. There is no point appealing to the conscience of an evil man, for he has none.

479. We can be aware of evil and yet not be frightened by it.

FACTS ABOUT FEELINGS

480. A dozen emotions will tell you why you should not take the true way, and all of them are betrayers.

481. Artificial happiness cannot be felt as real.

482. An action based on right thoughts will awaken right feelings.

483. You can turn sour feelings into healing powers.

484. A man succeeded in appearing right before other people, but it did nothing to make him feel right before himself.

485. Attraction to truth includes a higher feeling of rightness.

486. Remember that useless emotions will always insist that they are necessary.

487. The wrong harbor feels wrong, while the right harbor feels right.

488. Unawareness of a problem deceives us into thinking we are free of it, but our fearful feelings are not deceived.

489. If you no longer wish to feel divided you are feeling something right.

WHY SELF-DECEPTION MUST GO

490. Self-deception is not ten times greater but a thousand times greater than a man or woman realizes.

491. Man has the ruthless habit of truth-twisting.

492. The only thing worse than letting others tell you what you want to hear is to tell yourself what you prefer to hear.

493. Few burdens are heavier than a pretense of caring for others, which is lifted by daring to study the burden.

494. Perception and deception do not mix.

495. Like walking in a circle, contrived activities supply mere action without a satisfying purpose.

496. New external scenery creates the temporary illusion of new internal scenery.

497. Falsehood provides false comfort, which is why foolish people remain prisoners of falsehood.

498. Deception deceives the deceiver.

499. A man can tell himself a thousand lies, but none are capable of making him feel right.

500. People are as nervous as butterflies in a storm, never realizing that they themselves have caused the storm.

501. If truth wanted to be very blunt with a man or woman it could ask, "Who are you trying to kid?"

502. The more painful the self-deception the more we repress and deny it.

503. Self-centered imagination deceives billions of human beings into believing they know what life is all about.

504. There is no way to convince unhappy emotions that they are happy, but there is a way out of the dreadful drama.

LET SELF-TRANSFORMATION OCCUR

505. Pain and disappointment with outer life is a preliminary necessity for seeking inner life.

506. Only a changed comprehension of life changes anything.

507. Let a higher fact be what it wants to be and it will change you into what you want to be.

508. Asking for help while demanding to remain as we are is like boarding a ship but tying it to the dock.

509. The change within is subtle but definite.

510. Inner development proceeds as swiftly as the individual voluntarily surrenders wrong methods of development.

511. Make even one real inner conquest, and you will feel how it differs from conquest in society.

512. We might as well settle it once and for all that there is no way out except self-change through self-study.

STRANGE AND INCREDIBLE FACTS

513. How strange that man rarely wonders whether life has a meaning higher than politics or football games.

514. One hardened delusion is to believe that we can uplift conditions while not uplifting the mind.

515. There is a new life, but the old life has no interest in even investigating it.

516. Folly feels nervous in the company of wisdom, and to relieve its distress it calls wisdom folly.

517. Many people approach an authentic teacher with the smug assumption they know more than the teacher.

518. Nothing is more incredible than hearing human beings screaming about freedom while destroying each other.

519. Some people actually feel guilty at saying *no* to someone trying to deceive them!

520. Neurosis fears what it demands.

521. Peculiar man is hurt and baffled when truth asks him to think and act differently.

522. The chief occupation of human sickness is to manufacture more sickness.

523. It is an incredible scene to witness a man stand there and blame other people for his rude behavior.

524. You could live for years next door to an awakened person and get nothing from him unless you really wanted it.

525. How peculiar that people think they can have personal rescue without personal participation in their rescue.

526. Human beings can angrily insist they are not angry.

527. A sheep who does not know he is a sheep foolishly mistakes the wolf for the shepherd.

528. We resist being hoaxed by others, but eagerly invite hoaxes perpetrated by our own muddled minds.

529. Human beings ascribe human characteristics to their gods and then worship *that*!

530. A captive of an artificial conscience secretly hates it.

531. Arrogance occupies the peculiar position of having no doubts, and yet having a thousand doubts.

532. Man believes he is trapped in a corner, never looking up to see the open window above his head.

VICTORY OVER PAINFUL THOUGHTS

533. Confused thought is like a ship on iceberg patrol that runs into one.

534. Confined beliefs cannot create a spacious life.

535. You need do nothing with unpleasant thoughts but see and drop them.

536. Man's ignorance and fear create the very conditions he cannot understand and which he fears.

537. Wrong ideas are pirates dressed as noblemen.

538. We fear we might be wrong about something, not seeing that conceding wrongness makes us both right and free of fear!

539. One way to escape our own hauntings is to deliberately dare to let other people feel superior to us without fighting them.

540. Ignorance fears its own behavior.

541. A captured mind is one that insists, usually with anger, that it knows exactly what it is doing.

542. Higher consciousness has power to speak to and subdue tormenting thoughts.

SELF-CONQUEST AND SELF-COMMAND

543. Make every appearance of discomfort your signal for winning insight into it.

544. When ruling one's own life there is no desire to rule others.

545. If our present ways do not supply self-command it makes sense to drop them for ways that do.

546. Self-liberty can begin by seeing that self-flattering labels *are* mere labels, not realities.

547. Transcend your own life.

548. You must live with yourself and I must live with myself, which makes it clear where each of us must work.

549. See the difference in quietly studying a difficulty and letting it carry you away.

550. What is higher than yourself is not fearful of yourself.

551. Much depends upon whether we habitually criticize others or habitually examine ourselves.

552. Rightness is attractive only to what is right in us.

553. Notice that when you are in command of yourself you casually command exterior conditions.

554. Refuse to fall under the power of petty annoyances.

555. Human beings are like dethroned kings and queens who must recover their kingdoms.

556. Use a breakdown for a breakthrough.

557. Work at subtraction, for example, a student could subtract his wish to appear knowledgeable.

558. Remind yourself that you are made to conquer, but conquer according to spiritual standards.

REMEMBER YOUR REAL NATURE

559. Discover who you really are—and change everything!

560. A man's haunted house is constructed from the hundreds of mere ideas he has about himself, such as being either good or bad.

561. You are what you are, not what you think you are.

562. Nothing is happier or healthier than to see that one does not exist as the self-described person he imagined he was.

563. Remember your cosmic nature and you instantly pull the pain out of any condition.

564. A victory for vanity is a defeat for essence.

565. You need not obey harmful impulses, for your real nature does not do so.

566. A person is always true to his own nature, for he *is* his nature, still, his nature can change and rise.

567. True encouragement is simply your own real nature vibrating happily after a period of receptivity to truth.

568. When really trusting truth it never occurs to us to ask where it is taking us.

569. Real initiative consists of awareness of and oneness with your inner cosmic energy as it expresses itself outwardly.

570. Consider it a great day when you first glimpse a harmful attitude you never before realized had chained you.

571. Think from truth about life, not from life about truth.

572. When a million people declare that wrong is right, listen only to your cosmic integrity which knows better.

573. Only released truth within can be impressed by expressed truth without.

574. Let supreme truth make your destiny and thereby be free of anxious questions about your destiny.

575. True knowledge is the same as true confidence.

576. The capacity for remembering what you must do is increased by awareness that you cannot remember.

577. Life becomes clear as you watch what happens outside you as a result of what happens inside you.

578. Patiently let life happen as it wishes, for an anxious attempt to not miss anything makes you miss everything.

579. A problem has no relationship to your real nature.

580. Discovery increases with awareness that discovery is impossible as long as one already has fixed conclusions.

581. The intellect may ask a question, but a true answer must come from a higher level than the intellect.

582. A worry is trying to tell us that the mind is in the wrong place, like a king struggling in the wilderness instead of enjoying his throne.

PRINCIPLES FOR REFLECTION

583. A great secret is to use these facts to get interested in your life in *a completely new way.*

584. Refuse to accept anything that keeps us in the dark.

585. You do not desire something because it is good, instead, you label it as good because you desire it.

586. We need the wisdom to have nothing to say.

587. Hostile criticism is far from being the same thing as conscious judgment.

588. The mercy we need is self-mercy, which consists of ceasing to behave badly while justifying it.

589. Hearing truth is not the same as understanding it.

590. Real conscience arises from Cosmic Command, not from obeying man-made rules.

591. Ideas can be right or wrong, and only cosmic consciousness can select the right and reject the wrong.

592. In the name of truth we can do everything we cannot do in the name of error.

UNDERSTAND CONTRADICTIONS

593. Millions of people agree that world-change starts with self-change, but few will do it.

594. An example of self-contradiction is when a problem-causer sees himself as a problem-solver.

595. With perfectly serious faces men and women can sit around a large table and plan a war in order to insure peace.

596. Peculiar man fails to see how his public claim to rightness is contradicted by his private feeling of wrongness.

597. Try rising above opposing desires instead of choosing between them.

598. One freedom from contradiction comes as one frees himself of ideas he promotes but does not really believe.

599. Realize you cannot be one way and act another way without feeling conflict and contradiction.

600. A refusal to examine self-contradictions is a refusal to leave the dreadful self-dungeon.

601. Self-conflict and self-contradiction are the same painful condition.

602. People live in a peculiar position of protecting wrong ideas they cannot value because the ideas have no value except to egotism.

603. People fear losing a niceness they never had!

604. When a true teacher speaks firmly to those who wrongly idolize him, the idolators soon depart in scorn of the teacher.

605. People want peace while also wanting warring thoughts.

606. People cannot see contradictions, so those who wreck the world believe they can rebuild it.

607. An unwhole mind attributes wholeness to itself, thus lives in the pain of its own contradictions.

608. Observe the difference between a person's words and the expression on his face.

609. A person is his private thoughts, not his public speeches.

610. Wishing the benefits of truth without living in it is like remaining in shadows while wanting the warmth of sunshine.

PRACTICE SELF-CORRECTION

611. Everyone possesses an internal self-correction system to which he must connect himself.

612. Do not let the momentum of a mistake continue to carry you forward, but break it and correct it as soon as possible.

613. Pretending to want self-correction corrects nothing.

614. Badness is handled wrongly when fearing it, and rightly when examining it.

615. One way to delay inner healing is to wish to have and feel power over other human beings.

616. When your old nature behaves badly, let your new nature be aware of it.

617. False self-certainty shakes its possessor, but the very shaking is a guiding message to willing listeners.

618. Collect corrections.

619. We learn from a mistake only when trying to correct its cause within ourselves.

620. There is a much better thing to do than run away from our deliverance, which is to run toward it.

HOW TO SOLVE PROBLEMS

621. Like a skilled doctor, truth always knows the medicine you need for the particular problem.

622. Problems are ended by not referring everything back to the self, the false self.

623. Study a difficulty without being hypnotized by it.

624. The real problem in life is not what we fail to obtain but what we fail to comprehend.

625. Real and higher solutions are found by thinking, "Maybe my present viewpoint is the problem."

626. Cosmic consciousness never needs to solve problems because it does not create them in the first place.

627. When one dissolves his artificial personality he ceases to be a problem-creating machine.

628. To solve a problem you must know more than the problem.

629. A discussion of personal problems scares people more than they know, but it is essential to the cure.

630. The kind of mind that creates problems cannot solve them, for only a higher mind has solutions.

631. Drop the wrong thought and you lose the problem it creates.

632. If the mind whirls with a problem, the only real problem is the whirling, which self-work can correct.

633. The right turn is to turn within.

634. Remaining bluffed by the false power of a problem is half the problem.

635. Conditioned thinking appears to settle a problem, when it merely replaces it with a second problem.

636. An awakened mind can explain all problems clearly because it is not a part of them.

PROOFS AND GUARANTEES

637. You need not prove to yourself or others that enlightenment is possible, but need only let the light itself prove it.

638. Confirm these truths by personal experience.

639. The perfect proof of rightness is the absence of the anxious need to prove itself to oneself or others.

640. Believe what you can see with your own spiritual eyes.

641. Dare to prove yourself wrong about something, then notice how it releases the light of rightness.

642. Every point in this book can be personally checked and proved by you, the reader.

HOW TO DESTROY FEAR

643. By having the honesty to see how easily we get scared we can gain the power to not get scared.

644. Have no fear in thinking about things you fear to think about, for eventual consciousness will end the fear.

645. Remember that suppressed fear is still frightening.

646. Fear must be conquered, for action based in fear will only produce more fear.

647. Self-knowledge has total power over vague dreads.

648. Fear cannot invade without the unconscious permission of the fearful.

649. Do not fear your fear.

650. Fearing truth is simply the wrong response of false ideas, for truth cannot fear itself.

651. Fear cannot hear anything higher than itself.

652. Fear is kept alive only by imagining that it is necessary to psychic survival, which it is not.

653. When someone throws a fearful idea at you, refuse to catch it.

654. Fear is caused by protecting false positions, so where there is no false position to defend there is no fear.

655. Smugness is a kind of unconscious dread.

656. Do not give life to weakness by fearing it, and it will gradually fade away for lack of support.

SELF-DEFEATING BEHAVIOR

657. One kind of self-defeating behavior is to refuse to examine self-defeating behavior.

658. If anyone wants his own way he can have it, after which he need only live with its pain.

659. Can we plant mental weed seeds and expect beautiful flowers?

660. Self-defeating behavior is encouraged by rewarding it, perhaps with false sympathy or by justifying it.

661. Feeling good over another person's disgrace is a wrong way to feel good.

662. All forms of self-defeating behavior are unseen, unconscious, which is why their existence is denied.

663. Man writes his own book of fiction and then complains about its many tragedies.

664. The one way to end the damage of self-defeating behavior is to stop the self-defeating behavior.

665. The person responsible for the self-damaging reaction to an event is the one who makes the reaction.

666. Self-defeating behavior fades out of our day as we rise above intellectualism to Cosmic Command.

REAL MENTAL POWER

667. A wise mind uses wrong experiences to create right knowledge which ends wrong experiences.

668. Mental silence is the perfect response to a challenge.

669. Your objective is to be as aware of your mental processes as you are of outer processes.

670. Free the mind and free the life.

671. Practice calling your mind back from past and future to attend to the present moment.

672. A mind in light sees everything right.

673. The developed deeper mind can observe surface thoughts and make needed corrections.

674. Right thoughts are the jewels in the cosmic crown.

675. Deliberately slow down the pace of the mind, for this creates a clearness impossible to mental panic.

676. A wise mind lets every idea prove itself right or wrong.

677. No one needs to be a famous philosopher in order to think rightly, but needs only the wish to command the day.

678. Extraordinary wisdom exists above the ordinary mind.

679. You really know something when knowing it completely from yourself, needing no support from others.

680. Think thoughtfully.

681. The more truth you can take the more you will command your own mind and the less it will command you.

682. Having mechanical duties only during the day is strain and boredom, but conscious actions make it a great day.

683. Never fear your misunderstanding, but patiently teach it.

684. When dealing with people in any situation remember that you are dealing with lazy minds which love habitual responses.

685. A silent mind actually sees what a noisy mind pretends to see.

686. Take as your powerful thought that the way out of the human jungle exists!

THE VALUE OF SHOCKS

687. Rightly used, shocks can teach you to be shockless.

688. Use shocks rightly by letting them fall on a wish to perceive, not on a wrong area, such as hurt feelings.

689. Slow down and finally stop wounded vanity from asserting itself after a shocking humiliation.

690. When we avoid the jolt of hearing the facts about ourselves we avoid our own wholeness.

691. A jolt indicates we had carelessly taken the sleeping state as the awakened state.

692. If you have an idea as to what is good and right for your life, let it be shaken thoroughly.

693. Jolts taken with a wish to learn the lessons from them will replace vanity with humility.

694. A shock to self-esteem can teach self-awakening.

695. Accept the shocks of seeing yourself as you are, and you can then accept the shocks of seeing others as they really are.

696. If shock is the only lesson we can understand, then we must welcome shock.

697. A jolt taken rightly supplies the wisdom to see that we did not know what we assumed we knew.

698. If you want to know what you need to learn, it is what shocks you to learn.

PEACE AND CALM

699. Real peace has nothing to do with international agreements, but only with personal trueness.

700. Authentic wisdom is one with calmness.

701. The shock of seeing what we are fades away in the peace of being who we are.

702. Doing what is truly right is frightening at first, but later becomes calm and effortless.

703. Let yourself flow forward casually.

704. Your own lack of strain does much to take the strain out of your human relationships.

705. Calmness is increased by seeing the connection between insincerity and nervousness.

706. The higher inner world is always peaceful and pleasant.

TRUTHS ABOUT HAPPINESS

707. Happiness exists when the inner man rules outer things, while unhappiness exists when the outer rules the inner.

708. A person can be satisfied *with* himself only *from* himself.

709. Seek truth, not happiness, then see how your ideas about happiness change drastically.

710. You are happy when your real nature casually lives out your day for you.

711. Any teaching which tries to make you happy with yourself as you now are must be strictly avoided.

712. Happiness happens when thoughts yield themselves to the wisdom of Cosmic Command.

713. It is no more necessary to think about happiness than it is to think about breathing.

714. What comes between you and happiness is you.

715. Happiness is the attained ability to live the rich life we are capable of living.

716. If we can paint the air, we can be happy with wrong ideas.

717. Unhappiness is a state in which internal areas are closed to a person by his ignorance.

718. Can one's happiness be real happiness if it causes pain to someone else?

719. The confining is the unhappy, the liberating is the happy.

720. You will eventually understand what it means to happily ignore the allures of the world.

721. Live from the internal foundation and all is well.

722. We have carelessly set aside the gift of happiness, but now we can take it through higher wisdom.

DEVELOP SPIRITUAL SIGHT

723. We act toward the world according to the way we see it, which is why clear sight is essential.

724. Like a fog, lack of insight stands between us and the view of our cosmic castle.

725. When not wanting to see a fact the right move is to go right ahead and see it.

726. Spiritual sight alone can see the difference between society's hero and a cosmic hero.

727. The mind finds treasures beyond itself by not assuming that what it now sees is all that exists.

728. See with a clear mind for just one second, and you dissolve the difficulties of all past years.

729. What you want is right in front of you at this very moment, so develop your inner eyesight.

730. If you really see the ailment, you will really see the medicine.

731. Personal insight is like having a well of pure water on your own property, instead of depending upon a pipe from outside.

732. The entire spiritual journey can be summarized in the counsel, "Look until you see."

VANITY AND CONCEIT

733. Vanity consists of a self-pleasing picture one has of himself, but which shakes nervously because it is unreal.

734. Notice how self-idolization is unconscious of itself, as with people who talk about themselves endlessly.

735. Conceit is nervous, suspicious, on guard, never at rest.

736. Just to see the pain and strain in vanity is enough to make us want to live without it.

737. Can we expect decency from anyone who calls his neurosis strength or leadership or decisiveness?

738. Imagination based in vanity is not intuition.

739. Higher hearing develops by realizing a present incapacity for hearing, which is a right blow against vanity.

740. Vanity cannot hear anything that threatens its position.

741. Praising our conceits is like complimenting a pack of vicious wolves.

742. Egotism is tortured by the endless need to distort facts.

743. Nervous haste is often a form of vanity which boasts, "See how many important tasks cry for my attention!"

744. Vanity is a prominent feature in gullibility.

745. The wrong road is crowded with travelers because it never requires the sacrifice of cunning conceit.

746. The very idea that others may know more about right living than we do is unacceptable to vanity.

747. Self-centeredness cannot see itself as self-centered.

748. Nothing good can come from learning intended as a vanity-serving ornament.

749. Vanity can be seen as poison only after a crisis forces us to abandon it even a little.

750. We possess only those realities we have earned by accepting hundreds of humiliations to our vanities.

HELPFUL EXPLANATIONS

751. One aim of a real teacher is to help his students become their own teachers.

752. If you want a noble and rewarding task in life, wish to and try to understand yourself.

753. The weakness of another person is no excuse for falling apart.

754. Final surrender to God, Truth, is to realize there is really no personal self to surrender.

755. Real wisdom is real security.

756. Does it make sense to help an oppressed group so that it can in turn become the oppressor?

757. Anyone who rejects truth will always lie about his reason for doing so.

758. Nothing pleases hostile spirits.

759. Interrupt wild thoughts with the realization that they are not necessary, which gradually weakens their false power.

760. It is always right to think, "By trying to understand this crisis I will be inwardly richer when it is over."

PLEASANTNESS

761. Most human pleasantness is simply the handy method by which one person gets what he wants from someone else.

762. Suppressed hostility is not pleasantness.

763. Real pleasantness toward oneself and others is composed of the individual's healthy thoughts.

764. If one is authentically pleasant toward himself he will be authentically pleasant toward others.

765. To be truly spiritual is to be truly pleasant.

766. Pleasantness arising from Cosmic Command is constant, for it does not depend upon good fortune.

INNER NEWNESS

767. As birds tell weary sailors of nearby land, true ideas foretell a new life.

768. Have no fear of exposing the illusion that your present world is a false world, for the end of the old reveals the new.

769. Wishing for something other than darkness is already a bit of light.

770. Enter yourself, let self-honesty turn you in the right direction, after which self-awareness lives your life for you.

771. The whole idea is to drink from your own fountain of released wisdom.

772. Your day is as new as you are.

773. Change starts with even the dim realization of being betrayed by our own faulty thoughts.

774. Increase your ability to be impressed by the new and true.

775. To travel from knowing spiritual facts to living them we must pass through the vanity of knowing.

776. Self-renewal occurs spontaneously when habitual thoughts are dropped.

777. Newness is obtained by dropping what is called certainty for what you imagine is uncertainty.

778. Right obedience is to obey your yearning for newness.

779. The reckless running of old thoughts prevents the appearance of new ways.

780. Few people realize how little truth they can take, but those who do will become new.

781. Declare, "I need not remain as I am" and then proceed to turn that fact into a personal experience.

ESCAPES AND DISTRACTIONS

782. The inner quest succeeds only if the seeker does not relieve his pain with escapes and distractions.

783. A god or idol created by anxious thought can do nothing for you.

784. Criticizing everyone else on earth for every fault he has does not elevate the criticizer one inch.

785. Complaint against others really says, "How terrible that you do not confirm my illusions about myself."

786. Pretense of wisdom fearfully refuses to look at itself.

787. You can associate with slaves who call themselves free, or you can associate with Cosmic Command and be free.

788. Noise plays an important part in hypnotic human affairs, as when loud music distracts from self-awareness.

789. Forsake fantasy.

790. Truth does not hide from anyone, which means that it is men and women who hide.

791. The attractions of the outer world seem fascinating only because we do not yet know the real fascination of the inner world.

KEYS TO UNDERSTANDING

792. Cosmic understanding is real magic, for it can change an endured life into a light life.

793. Just to see that acquired opinions are not the same as true understanding is already a great gain.

794. Quoting a truth is far from the same as understanding and living it.

795. We choke from our own smoke.

796. Ignorance is to see only the small part of the picture revealed by self-interest, while imagining we see the whole.

797. Insight starts with a wish to have it, then develops by taking the necessary internal actions.

798. Uplift understanding.

799. When really understanding a spiritual truth you simply live it without thinking about it.

800. The departure from assumptions is the same as the approach toward understanding.

801. Hearing must always come before understanding.

802. Reaching conclusions is a lower form of thinking which takes time, but cosmic comprehension is immediate.

803. It is wrong to think that goodness and understanding reside in whatever agrees with our preferred beliefs.

804. Understand your reactions by slowing them down.

805. It is quite possible to not understand an idea and yet not be afraid of your lack of understanding.

806. It is never necessary to worry over something you cannot understand.

807. The simple alternative to worry is to remain receptive to a force higher than misunderstanding.

808. An individual always experiences whatever he is, and nothing else.

809. A man comprehends an offered truth only when it causes an echo within himself.

810. Cynicism about human badness is not the same as seeing it from a whole and comprehending mind.

811. Never mind how long you must study an idea before understanding it, for the longer the run the longer the leap.

THE FOLLY OF INTELLECTUALISM

812. The intellect must work in its right room in the cosmic castle, and not imagine it is the whole castle.

813. Intellectualism causes its own anxiety by trying to prove that the untrue is true.

814. So-called intellectuals are always in trouble with their emotions.

815. Using mechanical thought to stop human destruction is as useless as trying to stop time by smashing a clock.

816. Isolation is the pain of intellectualism.

817. Intellectualism is one of the last walls to fall before the individual enters his liberty beyond the walls.

818. There is much more to your life than ordinary thoughts can describe.

819. Intellectualism lacks self-awareness, which means that the intellectual has no control of his inner life.

820. Inform your intellect that a higher wisdom exists above it.

821. Lessons in goodness fall first on the intellect, but must go higher than that for goodness to exist.

THE PROBLEM OF JEALOUSY

822. Envy arises from comparison, and comparison arises from the illusion of having a separate self which must compete in order to "prove" its existence.

823. Only the false self compares itself with others and becomes jealous, so end jealousy by ending the false self.

824. Look at the scared faces of people you envy, then see whether you still envy them.

825. Living in truth is the same as living in self-completion, which contains no jealousy.

826. Painful envy is an excellent place to begin to say *no* to inward foreign invaders.

827. Envy and feeling cheated in life are wrong attitudes which Cosmic Command can correct.

828. The good fortune of other people has absolutely no connection with your own liberty and happiness.

829. We need do only one thing with envy and other unhappy states, which is to understand and end them.

CHEERFUL THOUGHTS

830. You are being nice to yourself in a very special way when studying these ideas.

831. Every situation is a learning situation to an eager learner.

832. Anyone who chooses to live in a higher world can do so by listening to and submitting to the higher world.

833. The more you drink from the fountain of truth the more you want to drink.

834. What you are trying to do for yourself can be done.

835. Think rightly about yourself and you will have no concern as to what others think about you.

836. We can never be too eager toward self-discovery.

837. Any message saying you need not be afraid is a true and beautiful message.

838. Live lightly.

839. Walk forward while still in shadows and you will finally reach the sunshine.

840. Nothing is more generous than truth.

841. The very effort to understand something includes the right feeling that all is well.

AVOID MISTAKES AND GRIEFS

842. Do not assume that an idea is wrong just because it is not presently understood.

843. There is such a thing as wrong seriousness, as when worrying about being liked by others.

844. Failure to study your psychological territory results in sailing upstream to run into a waterfall.

845. It is easier to condemn our neighbor's house than to put our own house in order.

846. We should be glad to see where we are going wrong.

847. When a wrong act is truly understood, it expresses itself with calm feeling, "I will not do *that* again."

848. Live in single rightness and you will not be caught in conflict between two errors.

849. If someone else can drink our own water for us, then someone else can perform our own spiritual tasks.

850. We need not choose a self-damaging reaction.

851. You have a right to live your own life, and also have the responsibility for making it a harmless life.

852. Do not obey demanding distractions which try to lure you away from Cosmic Command, for they have no real power over you.

853. We wrongly think our problems into existence.

854. Seeking the answers to life on the intellectual level alone is like seeking the sun on the ocean floor.

855. Lazy assumptions are hazardous, as when thinking a man's outer niceness is matched inwardly.

856. Welcome painful correction.

857. We stop playing the painful social game when clearly seeing it as a disastrous game.

858. Pay *consciously* for a mistake and we end both the mistake and the payment.

859. We pay consciously for a mistake by letting awareness of the error destroy a bit of self-conceit.

SELF-TEACHING IS A PLEASURE

860. We can learn to run as fast to inner help as we may now run to outer aid.

861. Freely tell yourself about yourself.

862. Investigate what it means to no longer be a victim of oneself.

863. You are not required to believe anyone who tells you he knows the truth, for self-discovery alone is real.

864. Solitude instructs as nothing else can do.

865. Instead of trying to change other people, change your own thinking toward them.

866. Value vigilance.

867. Our hurts try to show us where we are calling a marsh a meadow.

868. Make it your happy aim to get through to yourself.

869. When making a mistake, try to connect it with a lack of clear thinking.

FACTS ABOUT THE MIND

870. What you really need to know is how the mind works, for as the mind goes, so goes the life.

871. Anyone can learn how to possess his own mind.

872. A clear idea in print rightly excites the part of you that is struggling to be clear.

873. The mind needs right direction as much as your car.

874. A true idea causes discomfort only because it falls on a wrong part of the receiving mind.

875. False attitudes are denied because they are unconscious.

876. A clear mind is a king.

877. A right thought is simply one that does not cause trouble to the thinker or anyone else.

878. It is a man's own thought that connects him, rightly or wrongly, with other people and events.

879. The mind can know itself.

880. Wrong ideas create a weird sort of self-idolization, like a man worshipping his trashy house.

881. Incorrect thinking robs the incorrect thinker.

882. Mechanical thought takes up space which should be rightly occupied by consciousness.

883. Mechanical thinking has no logic, much like a hand continuing to write when reaching the end of the paper.

884. We are replacing amateur thinking with professional thinking.

885. Cosmic insight is as high above ordinary logic as a sailing ship is above the ocean floor.

GUIDING THOUGHTS

886. A lesson is as clear as we permit it to be, so give your full permission.

887. The only reason the cosmic shepherd does not find the straying sheep is because it does not want to be found.

888. There is no way to explain real self-protection to anyone who refuses to listen to the explanation.

889. Cosmic Command contains no anxiety, for it is quietly content to remain with its own natural wholeness.

890. Assumption is laziness posing as fact.

891. You can let an accusation correct you, but you must never allow it to make you feel guilty and afraid.

892. You can have companions on the higher path, but only after mentally leaving those who do not want the path.

893. Anyone who does not want to grow will not want you to grow.

894. Work with these guides to end the painful feeling that you are not valued enough by other people.

895. Only the false self feels rejected, which means that your oneness with Cosmic Command can never feel rejected.

HAVE HEALTHY AIMS

896. Have the noble aim of learning what it means to be truly conscious, then be it.

897. Aim for harmony among all your parts, including feelings, ideas, words, actions and reactions.

898. Each time you insist you know what is best for you, ask why you need to insist.

899. Keep your right aims alive in yourself, and if they doze, shake them awake.

900. Aim for essentials, such as insights into your mind.

901. Inquire constantly, "What would be a truly different way to respond to life?"

QUESTIONS TO ASK YOURSELF

902. Might I unconsciously attract what I experience?

903. What are my present attitudes toward life and what kind of life have they produced?

904. What stands between me and the true view?

905. Do my favorite beliefs really conquer anxiety?

906. What difference does it make to my true interests if another person is a villain or a hypocrite?

907. How fast can I unlearn what I have taken as learning?

908. Could my betrayal be self-betrayal?

909. Why make a fall necessary by climbing up the treacherous mountain of human schemes?

910. What kind of life can a man or woman have as long as confusion is in control?

911. How much of my life is wrongly determined by external influences?

912. Why cry?

913. Does anything really matter except to have inner wholeness?

THE DESERT OF EGOTISM

914. Getting through human self-centeredness is like trying to push a marshmallow through a brick wall.

915. Egotism insists that its miserable world is the only world that exists or has a right to exist.

916. Egotism is the illusory belief that labels, experiences, habits and possessions constitute a real and permanent self.

917. Ego-defense supplies the false pleasure of agitation, which is wrongly taken as evidence of the existence of the ego.

918. A chief feature of egotism is its wrong and cunning belief that it possesses an individual identity apart from the Whole.

919. Self-centeredness knows no viewpoint but its own, though it craftily pretends to see outside of itself.

920. Egotism changes its appearance, but never its trickery.

921. The social ship sinks because everyone claims to be its rightful captain.

922. A principal task of egotism is to distort truth, and one method is to call truth egotism.

923. Egotists can give brilliant lectures on humility.

924. Evil egotism eagerly pounces upon another man's evil, while decency is free of pouncing.

925. When self-centeredness explains why it does something it always lies.

926. The fear in egotism is evident when it demands, "Love me or hate me, but do not ignore me."

927. A person who cannot enlighten himself will be quite sure he can enlighten the world.

928. Egotism can put on a thousand different faces in pretending it wants the light, but it loves only its own darkness.

929. Self-glorification fears derision.

930. Egotism's level of intelligence is revealed when it sneers at everything truly right and decent.

931. A man who boasts about his independence is very dependent upon telling you this.

932. Self-centeredness is incapable of learning a lesson from an experience, having only a wish to feel a neurotic thrill.

933. The ousting of unseen egotism is a fundamental principle of every true teaching.

LEVELS OF COMPREHENSION

934. High or low, the level of our mind determines the nature of our experiences.

935. What seems good and logical to the ordinary mind is seen as harmful and absurd to the awakened mind.

936. Every spiritual idea can be seen in higher ways than the way we first take it.

937. Contact with truth reveals a person's actual nature, his high or low level of being.

938. Truth is never offended when we foolishly reject it, but it does firmly decline to come down to our level.

939. Lies and deceits may be part of a person's present level, but they are not permanent obstacles to a higher level.

940. Anything that forces you to look at life from a higher viewpoint is your friend.

941. To reach a higher level, slow down, calm down.

942. Remind yourself daily, "I see everything according to my *present* level of understanding."

943. Sensible and efficient work on the everyday level qualifies us for higher levels.

WEAKNESS AND EXHAUSTION

944. Be glad, not afraid, at the exhaustion of ego-strength, for now a higher power can enter and guide.

945. The trouble with neurosis is that it has no pauses.

946. If you wish to resign from life in the right way, resign from harmful beliefs which insist they are helpful.

947. When running out of strength, just keep going without it.

948. Boredom is caused by living only on the intellectual level, and is cured only by rising to Cosmic Command.

949. Nothing is more exhausting than artificial morality.

950. Strength or weakness depends upon the quality of the mental food we eat.

951. Truth should be sought because it is the only right home for the weary wanderer.

FREEDOM FROM TROUBLESOME PEOPLE

952. A tyrant has no power over you except as your misunderstanding sees him as a strong tyrant.

953. Do not fear a tyrant and you will see him tremble at the loss of his dramatic role as a tyrant.

954. If you invite people to take advantage of you, they will.

955. Do not let another person's bad behavior become your problem, but leave it with him, where it belongs.

956. If you sympathize with a rogue you had better watch your wallet.

957. Anyone who leads you into trouble will abandon you once his or her self-interest is satisfied.

958. Intimidation can be refused only when sharp insight into human nature recognizes it immediately.

959. By learning to not interfere with your own natural life-flow, you free yourself of interfering people.

960. A person is chained to others because he is not free of himself.

961. One good way to be deceived by people is to attribute illusory goodness to them.

962. You are free from someone when not wrongly and gullibly crediting him with goodness and strength.

963. You can be free of the fear of others getting angry with you.

964. When wanting something from the sheep, the wolf always insists he only wants to give something.

965. Whether aware of it or not, a deceived person consents to the outer deception by his inner confusion.

966. We have false friends because we give them false rewards.

967. Never let accusing people deceive you into thinking you must anxiously defend yourself against them.

968. Anyone who displays great emotional regret over hurting you will do it again.

969. People who wish to exploit you often start by sadly discussing how exploited you are.

970. Do not be inwardly attached to troublesome people.

971. You can learn to be independent and uninfluenced by the negative moods of other people.

GUIDES FOR STUDY GROUPS

972. Meet regularly at a time and place of maximum convenience for the majority of students.

973. Urge everyone to arrive on time, but make allowances for those whose schedule makes it difficult.

974. A small donation may be requested per member at each meeting to pay for expenses.

975. Some may wish to take notes, while others may prefer to give full attention to listening.

976. Courtesy and orderliness, such as one person speaking at a time, is a sign of group-intelligence.

977. Do not become stiffly organized, but keep the class light and informal, with a friendly atmosphere.

TEACHINGS ABOUT GOODNESS

978. Goodness understands badness, but badness does not understand goodness.

979. Badness calls itself goodness, therefore it cannot understand real goodness.

980. Love even a small amount of goodness, and more will be given.

981. It takes a truly moral man or woman to simply leave other people alone.

982. Goodness seeking benefit is artificial goodness.

983. There exists a natural goodness which never needs to think about itself.

984. Real kindness grows only from real enlightenment.

985. Eagerly pouncing on the badness of others will never make the pouncer good.

986. Goodness received from outside will not last unless it is received by goodness inside.

987. Self-wholeness is effortless goodness.

ALL ABOUT WORDS

988. Words coming from a conscious mind have healing power for those who hear and understand.

989. Anyone satisfied with pretty words is dissatisfied with his unpretty life.

990. Saying we want inner rescue is not the same as meaning it.

991. Remember the key word of *release,* for example, release the refreshing flow of the inner spring.

992. There is lofty communication between a real teacher and a real student, which may or may not include words.

993. Notice how much of human talk is senseless, compulsive, mechanical, unconscious, impolite—and endless.

994. Those having few facts use many words.

995. Truth is not on the level of words, which is why it is easier to see truth than explain it.

996. Realize that any word, such as *rightness,* has a dozen different meanings to a dozen people.

997. Men pin labels on what they fail to understand, then think they see it, for example, human hostility is handled by forming a committee for "peace and brotherhood."

998. Just as a map of a town is not the town itself, a word is not the reality it represents.

999. Nothing is more generous with itself than nonsensical blab.

1000. Our condition reacts wrongly to mere words, but our essence does not, for it sees words as mere words.

1001. One of the most important words to remember as you study is the word *authentic*.

1002. Words are tools for building boats to cross the river, but words must not be seen as the boats themselves.

1003. A distorted mind always speaks a distorted message.

1004. We must learn the meaning behind words, like a lost child able to understand street signs.

1005. Words arising from Cosmic Command will be right, while words coming from the invented self will be wrong.

POINTS TO PONDER

1006. A teacher never struggles with a wrong question, but tries to make the student aware that it is a wrong question.

1007. There is no way to protect from themselves those who do not want protection from themselves.

1008. Be in right service to yourself.

1009. One benefit of self-wholeness is that you need not go anywhere to find what you need.

1010. The same truth that taught you will show you how and where to teach others.

1011. Rejection contains an artificial thrill, as with false teachers who love to claim persecution.

1012. Spiritually, we get by giving up.

1013. True conscience is the ability to see evil without unconscious involvement in it, like an innocent man observing a criminal.

1014. A man is what his face says he is when he is temporarily tired of pretending.

1015. Self-examination and self-transformation should be your daily aims simply because they are good for you.

NATURALNESS

1016. A river has no purpose except to flow easily, according to its own nature, which is also our natural purpose.

1017. A natural individual easily handles unnaturalness in others.

1018. At first you must urge your mind forward with right ideas, but later it flows by itself, easily, naturally.

1019. It is natural to not want to be with unnatural people.

1020. Natural action is developed by becoming aware of forced behavior, such as detecting forced cheerfulness.

1021. Natural behavior is effortlessly warm and friendly.

LIVE YOUR OWN FREE LIFE

1022. Suggestibility is conquered by submitting every inner and outer suggestion to the judgment of Cosmic Command.

1023. End self-division by doing what is right for your true life, not what others insist is right for you.

1024. We can learn to be ourselves by not fearing and resisting the newness of it.

1025. Belong to yourself.

1026. It is a warm act, not a cold one, to place rightness ahead of your relatives.

1027. Your task is responsibility for your own inner development, regardless of the irresponsibility of others toward themselves.

1028. An individual can see life with borrowed opinions or with his own spiritual eyesight.

1029. Wishing to appear loving or generous or brave before other people prevents one from living his own life.

1030. Do not allow interfering people to waste your life.

1031. To truly have a life of his own an individual must voluntarily abandon what he now calls a life of his own.

1032. Do not expect your friends to applaud if you decide to stop playing society's shallow games.

1033. True independence, and Oneness with the All, are the same thing.

WHY PEOPLE FAIL

1034. Most people crave to be told it is not their fault, which is why most people remain in pain.

1035. The last thing a childish mind wants to hear is that it is childish.

1036. Fear must continue as long as a man hides among other hiders.

1037. It is easier to teach arithmetic to an ape than to teach sincerity to a dreamer who imagines he is already sincere.

1038. Few men want to listen to even fewer wise men.

1039. Having intellectual ideals is simply a cunning evasion of the true task of erasing egotism.

1040. Thrill the vanity and weaken the life, which is not simply a moralistic statement but a solid spiritual law.

1041. No one sees a truth he does not want to see.

1042. Do you think people really want to see what a bad relationship they have with themselves?

1043. A thousand angels cannot get through to anyone living in imagination masquerading as insight.

DESCRIPTIONS OF HOSTILE THOUGHTS

1044. They insist it is your moral duty to help others, then when others betray you they sit back and laugh at your gullibility.

1045. They rejoice when goodness appears to be hurt.

1046. They insist that confusion is necessary, and demand that you try to prove they are wrong.

1047. They build up painful pressure, then say it is all right to explode against and hurt others.

1048. They tell you it is clever or heroic to behave in a certain way, then accuse you of stupidity for doing so.

1049. They force you to pretend interest in trivial events or nonsensical solutions to life, then leave you exhausted.

1050. They love to predict and talk about calamities, causing terror and physical violence.

1051. They supply bad advice for helping yourself, and when you take it they claim you are too gullible to ever save yourself.

1052. They secretly sneer at everyone they pretend to love.

1053. They torment you with suspicion and then claim that suspicion is intelligent and necessary.

1054. They sneak evil thoughts into your mind and then threaten you with punishment for having them.

1055. They cunningly promise rich rewards for listening to them, then desert you to suffer alone with your false gains.

1056. They deceive you by implanting a false conscience by demanding your loyalty to dangerous people.

1057. The last thing they want you to see is their lack of real power over you, for they know it would be their finish.

COLLECT THESE HELPFUL IDEAS

1058. The truly unselfish person seeks to understand and rescue himself in order to have real value to give to others.

1059. Awareness of living from artificial personality ends the tyrannical self-punishment of artificial personality.

1060. Billions of so-called religious people take faith in their neurosis as faith in God.

1061. There is no burden quite so burdensome as artificial spirituality.

1062. Anyone who gets angry or upset when his beliefs are challenged has false beliefs.

1063. Deluded minds always call purposeless action purposeful action.

1064. What we often take as impressive intelligence in a stranger is simply a new kind of stupidity.

1065. Do not think that being subdued and suppressed is the same as being consciously quiet.

1066. Only fearless people can be pleasant at all times.

1067. Anyone looking for an excuse to reject truth will find one, even if he has to invent one.

1068. Sacrifice rightly by sacrificing the delusion of having something of value to sacrifice.

1069. A main aim of neurosis is to make noise, not sense.

1070. Let the tense face of a rude or angry person teach you that any negative state is its own punishment.

1071. A man has no incentive to seek real gold as long as he thinks his artificial gold is real.

RIGHT DEPENDENCY

1072. When you can no longer depend upon your present solutions, you can ask for and receive real solutions.

1073. Nervousness and doubt are caused by trying to depend upon the artificial self.

1074. Cosmic Command possesses a calm confidence unknown by usual thoughts.

1075. Depending upon wrong attitudes to solve a crisis is like asking bandits to protect your money.

1076. When living from inner trueness we no longer wearily depend upon acceptance from others.

1077. See the difference between depending upon calm wisdom and upon misleading emotions.

1078. Sooner or later, along the path, we see the need to submit personal thoughts to higher comprehension.

1079. Trust truth.

ACTIONS THAT SERVE YOU

1080. Life is always trying to express itself in action, and our part is to make the action naturally healthy.

1081. You do what you do because you are what you are.

1082. Only Cosmic Command can detect and dismiss the wrong motives we ascribe to wrong actions.

1083. Remembering right things keeps you doing right things.

1084. Facts given by a teacher must be turned into personal experience by a student.

1085. It can be called a right intention only if it goes into action.

1086. Perform an inner task simply because it is the right thing to do.

1087. It takes real intelligence to see the difference between impulsive and thoughtful action.

1088. Right actions do not cause wrong reactions.

1089. Knowledge without action is like sleeping in a library.

1090. Actions demanded by the tyrannical past drain strength, while actions flowing from the present moment add strength.

1091. See what must be done, then do it in spite of all inner protests.

1092. All *doing* should be directed toward being.

1093. Do not mentally linger over completed actions, but leave them and go on to the next fresh moment.

1094. Sour emotions hinder right action.

1095. Act for yourself, and one day you will act from yourself.

1096. An act which hurts another also hurts the doer of the act, for the doer is hurt by being a hurtful person.

1097. See the difference between strained and spontaneous action.

1098. Since fear can never act intelligently for us, it must be understood and dissolved.

1099. There is water in the human desert, but we must dig.

SELF-HONESTY AND SELF-SINCERITY

1100. Admitting a fault prevents the self-conflict which would have appeared had we denied it.

1101. Develop sincerity by questioning your sincerity.

1102. Agreeing that we are inwardly mixed up is not the same as agreeing to be made clear.

1103. One honest realization is to realize that we presently do not know what we want.

1104. Hide nothing, fear nothing.

1105. If just one small part of a person wants a new life, that is the perfect start for finding it.

1106. An insincere person convinces himself that necessary correction does not apply to *him*.

1107. Every insincere person is quite sure he is sincere.

1108. By admitting wrongness about something we take all the wrong fight out of it, and then begin to be right.

1109. Self-honesty follows the path of truth wherever it leads, even when it passes straight through inner storms.

FOLLOW THESE LOFTY TEACHINGS

1110. The one way to travel from anxiety to peace is to be willing to travel from the known to the unknown.

1111. Right desire is the wish to see things as they really are.

1112. Because evil is weak it will meet us halfway, but strong goodness never compromises.

1113. Seeking truth means to seek the truth about yourself.

1114. You rightly bear the weakness of another person by being conscious of it without submitting to it.

1115. The more you know you do not know, the more you know.

1116. A wasted day is one in which you fail to hear messages coming from a higher source than yourself.

1117. What is really right for you cannot be wrong for anyone else.

1118. You are in right relationship with another person when you want the truth for both that person and yourself more than you want the other person.

1119. No one needs to be a submissive victim of his own weakness.

1120. The first step in dropping dangerous delusions is to see that we do not deeply understand the meaning of that advice.

1121. There is no reply to viciousness, and none should be given.

1122. For inner peace or inner storm, you experience the results of your own daily choices.

1123. You are not required to think useless thoughts, so recognize and reject them.

1124. Be grateful for a power greater than you in the universe, which will do for you what you cannot do for yourself.

REFUSE TO BE INTIMIDATED

1125. When anyone tries to intimidate you, remember that intimidation is neurosis pretending it is power.

1126. Anyone who threatens you reveals himself as a scared weakling who need not be feared at all.

1127. A hostile spirit is always ready and eager to scream out in attention-attracting indignation.

1128. Some people enjoy intimidating others by displaying bad moods, but you must not fall for it.

1129. See a man who demands consideration from others and you see a man unable to give consideration to others.

1130. Refuse absolutely to be intimidated by anyone, anytime, anywhere, and if you weaken, refuse all over again.

CHARLATANS AND HYPOCRITES

1131. Two charlatans once met, and you never saw two men more eager to praise each other's honesty and goodness.

1132. Mass misery is caused by deluded leaders who insist they know how their actions will turn out.

1133. Hypocrites are surprised, bewildered and scornful at a lack of hypocrisy.

1134. False morality is like a thief whose honesty depends upon the bars in his cell.

1135. Deceivers laugh at their foolish followers.

1136. A charlatan first excites his target's imagination, then declares that it is not imagination but commendable reason.

1137. A flock of dejected sheep led meaningless lives, so they solved the problem by founding a school in which they taught other sheep how to lead meaningful lives.

1138. Only a truthful mind can help others, and all else is destructive hypocrisy.

1139. Being mechanical, a deceiver has no choice but to try to drag everyone else down to his own low level.

1140. Rascality loves sociality.

1141. Hypocrisy is quite willing to expose itself with evil gloating, once it has drained its gullible victim.

1142. If you want to know who you are, you must not believe that other people know what they are talking about when they tell you who you are.

FIND YOUR REAL SELF

1143. A wise plan for knowing who you are is to first discover who you are not, and you are not your acquired self-descriptions.

1144. Good or bad thoughts about yourself give you a self-description, but your description is not your true identity.

1145. Your true identity cannot be described with thoughts, but it can be lived with consciousness.

1146. Lose false identity and win true life.

1147. To be free of yourself really means to be free of every acquired and unconscious notion you have about yourself.

1148. When really knowing who you are you need not think about it, for you do not consist of thoughts about yourself.

1149. The less a man knows who he really is, the more he will frantically describe himself.

1150. There is nothing to fear in letting go of every idea you now have about yourself.

1151. Fear of seeing evil in oneself is false fear, for the fear is itself a part of the wrong self-identity.

1152. One's real identity is not that of either an evil or good person, but is an unlabeled expression of the Cosmic Whole.

1153. Never let other people tell you who you are.

1154. No one feels right with his imaginary identity.

1155. What prevents you from recognizing yourself is the hundreds of ideas which *call* themselves you.

1156. If you do not know who you are, remain in that state of unknowing, and the light will dawn.

1157. The pain of not knowing who you are is ended by seeing you need not be anyone at all.

1158. You will know who you are when having no *idea* of who you are.

1159. Anyone who falsely believes that his identity is at stake in a situation will have no conscience in that situation.

1160. Our true identity as part of the Cosmic Whole has no need for protection or promotion.

TENSION AND PRESSURE

1161. Tension, confusion and helplessness are caused by trying to live up to a flattering picture of oneself.

1162. Notice how tension talks in most people.

1163. The less you relieve the pressure with wrong ways the more you understand and end it with right ways.

1164. Pressure is not relieved by accusing others of having our own concealed faults.

1165. Pretense is tense.

1166. One way to remain tense is to depend upon others for pleasant feelings.

1167. Uncertainty is conquered by enduring it to the end, by refusing to relieve it with convenient answers.

1168. Get tired of tolerating tension.

HOW TO UNDERSTAND LIFE

1169. You understand something not by being for or against it, but by being above it.

1170. Have no fear in not having opinions on social questions, for that will finally create Cosmic Command.

1171. We are always fond of what we do, but it can be a harmful or beneficial fondness.

1172. Higher insight understands life-changes, like a viewer on a hill who sees why cars turn this way and that.

1173. The reason the world never solves its problems is because it never comes to the end of *its* solutions.

1174. Human laws do not change human nature.

1175. When worriedly thinking that other people are thinking bad thoughts toward you, the problem is your worried thinking.

1176. An event is understood the moment the self-centered mind stops trying for a self-centered interpretation.

1177. A million human events can happen, but unless they change human nature, nothing beneficial happens.

1178. Superstition is a weak mind's substitute for knowledge.

1179. Trying to force life to conform to personal cravings is like trying to build a statue out of water.

1180. We suffer from what we do not know about ourselves.

1181. Do not let people drag you into situations where you end up having to make the decisions and pay the money.

1182. Believing something to be true and good does not make it so.

1183. Hurt and humiliation are thrown into the world by those who can still be hurt and humiliated.

1184. Activate alertness.

1185. A small seed of your own understanding is worth more than a forest of theories offered by others.

1186. Discover what you truly value, for that is what makes your life whatever it is.

1187. We give a meaning to words, after which they give a right or wrong meaning to our actions.

1188. Since we unconsciously ask for our own grief, these ideas help us to stop asking.

ACTORS AND ACTRESSES

1189. Carefully watch the human tendency to be theatrical, to fondly play dramatic and unreal roles.

1190. Pretense is never quite so nervous as when it is pretending that it is not pretending.

1191. Seeing through society's stage performance does not change it, but it does keep you safe.

1192. Only an actor is deceived by the role of another actor.

1193. Nothing can be said to those who refuse to see they are merely pretending to know the answers.

1194. There is a great opportunity for anyone who is tired of pretending that all is well.

1195. Self-centered sentimentality is a type of human dramatics which tries to pass itself off as love or tenderness.

1196. The artificial self is incapable of decency, which it hides by praising decency.

1197. Pretending that we do not care about a personal loss can be replaced with actual liberty from it.

1198. Nothing can satisfy our deep yearnings but to be who we really are.

LEARNING THE LESSONS

1199. Give a lesson concentrated attention, then rest from it a bit and let natural light make things clear.

1200. The way to learn a lesson is to submit to it.

1201. A lesson may come first from a teacher or book, but then must come from the mind of the student.

1202. Treasure thoroughness.

1203. Truth wisely declines to let us proceed to a higher lesson before learning a lower lesson.

1204. When the dream-castle crashes, the sufferer has an opportunity to understand that it was made of dreams, not realities.

1205. An argumentative spirit cannot learn.

1206. Strong lessons are not meant to scare anyone, to the contrary, their purpose is to banish fright.

1207. A student is given strong or mild ideas, depending upon his ability to receive and absorb.

1208. Yearn to learn.

1209. Something wiser than you is trying to get through to you.

1210. Be willing to spend a thousand mental dollars to obtain one penny's worth of right cosmic instruction.

1211. Only unlearned lessons hurt.

1212. Higher wisdom is so overwhelmingly different that students can absorb only one small lesson at a time.

1213. Your next healthy lesson is on the other side of your next disappointment.

GOOD ADVICE

1214. When able to sight right advice from yourself you will also be able to follow and profit from it.

1215. Do not build your life upon what lost people tell you about life.

1216. Giving wrong advice to others is a good way to avoid acquiring right advice for oneself.

1217. Right advice is modest, while wrong advice is theatrical.

1218. Say silently to compulsive advisors, "I prefer to learn for myself, even if it means a thousand blunders."

1219. Something higher than the intellect can give quality advice, and that something is Cosmic Command.

FACTS ABOUT HUMAN NATURE

1220. When someone asks for your cooperation he usually means he wants you to do his work.

1221. Most people are complaint factories.

1222. There is no howl of indignation quite as loud as that of a persecuted persecutor.

1223. Society is fascinated by wrongness, not repelled by it.

1224. Being inwardly asleep means to live in fear, anger, tension and other negative states.

1225. In human affairs, the remedies are the maladies.

1226. Half the people are afraid that others will not understand their motives, and the other half are afraid they will.

1227. Contempt for others has no source but unseen self-contempt.

1228. Human beings do not understand even the simplest of facts, for example, that hatred burns the hater.

1229. Your good friends are not at all what they appear to be.

1230. Neurosis demands a reward for its neurosis!

1231. The life of most people is like a badly written story having so many twists and turns it cannot be followed.

1232. We assemble with those we resemble.

1233. Greed is simply a sign of defective self-knowledge in which the person imagines that possessions make him somebody.

1234. Most human beings spend their lives being true to the false.

1235. Anyone who tells you what you owe society is telling you what you owe *him*.

1236. Human moral standards are very immoral.

1237. You shock a critical person when asking him to supply something better than what he criticized.

THE INVISIBLE WORLD

1238. An invisible world of power and action exists just as certainly as the world seen by our senses.

1239. To even realize we do not think about the invisible world is a good introduction to it.

1240. The mental world you now inhabit is not the only world that exists.

1241. The kind of world you experience outwardly is the same kind of world you are inwardly.

1242. Build insight by realizing that the old ways *do not want to hear* the bright messages from the invisible world.

1243. To live in another world, be another world.

1244. One way to not discover the spacious world which can be discovered is to be a mental hermit.

1245. The real world does not have to be held together by frantic thought.

1246. Contact with the invisible world of wisdom supplies explanations unobtainable from the physical world.

1247. The rightness of the invisible world knows how to handle the wrongness of the exterior world.

TEACHER AND STUDENT RELATIONSHIPS

1248. Part of a teacher's task is to show students what they can do for themselves.

1249. An instructor is closer to the real nature of his students than the students themselves.

1250. The very manner of an awakened man is a lesson for those who can see it.

1251. A teacher appears as a fierce hawk to the stubborn, but as a gentle dove to those who want to learn.

1252. It might appear otherwise, but the only thing a teacher demands from his pupils is that they wake up.

1253. A real student is grateful when informed that he is thinking or talking or acting in his sleep.

1254. A real teacher deliberately jolts a real student, and both understand its healthy necessity.

1255. When a teacher of wisdom makes it hard on a student he is making it easier on the student.

1256. An instructor knows when a student's question is based in misunderstanding, and replies in a way to explain this.

1257. Anyone wanting to play the game of ego-competition with a teacher will be disappointed, for the teacher does not play the game.

1258. At certain times we think the teacher has just learned something new when it was ourselves that just learned!

1259. The right way to please a teacher is to first please truth.

1260. A teacher is not offended by a pupil's bad behavior, but not knowing this, the pupil may depart and lose his way.

1261. The slightest change in a student's facial expression tells the instructor what the student is hiding.

1262. A teacher's presence helps his pupil suspend his shadowy mind long enough for light to seep in.

1263. When an awakened man teaches, the atmosphere is loaded with learning.

1264. The healthy radiations of an awakened teacher can be felt only by those who are beginning to awaken.

1265. A teacher does not want his students to fawn before him, but he does expect correct behavior.

1266. A chief task of an instructor is to prevent a pupil from assuming he knows more than he does.

1267. A teacher speaks only to the positive attitudes in a student, while ignoring the negative parts.

PROCEED WITH QUIET PATIENCE

1268. The first fear you should drop is the fear of not succeeding at the inner task.

1269. If the fear of not succeeding comes back a thousand times you need only casually drop it a thousand times.

1270. Remember, anxiety over inner failure will fall away with your constant welcome of Cosmic Command.

1271. Let inner development proceed with no concern over the approval or disapproval of others.

1272. Act upon the fact.

1273. The patient gathering of an idea here or an insight there will build a solid inner residence.

1274. Glimpse this new way and you will not want to go back to the old ways.

1275. You should never give up, for truth never gives up on you.

ANGER AND HOSTILITY

1276. A major obstacle to be overcome is unseen and unadmitted hostility.

1277. A mind growing into new health habitually examines facts instead of angrily rejecting them.

1278. Fury toward yourself is a barrier toward understanding yourself.

1279. The winning of real wisdom and the fading of rage make progress alongside each other.

1280. Hostility is a harmful substitute for perception.

1281. Anyone can test how much he really knows by seeing if he gets hostile when told he understands nothing.

1282. The only thing that equals the popularity of anger is its uselessness.

1283. A hostile person fears the hostility of others.

1284. Human fury disconnects one from his enlightening power, like a home deprived of electricity by a storm.

1285. Concealed antagonism can never contain healing insight.

1286. A person becomes angry when told he is lying precisely because he is.

1287. A hostile person receives an ill thrill at scaring others, but you must refuse him this false reward.

1288. Hostility is in love with destruction.

1289. Anger fades as one sees it contributes only to the artificial self and is therefore harmful.

FAMILIAR AND UNFAMILIAR

1290. Daily life grows much better as you replace the familiar with the new.

1291. If you wish to reach a truly new goal, you must have no preconceived ideas about its nature.

1292. One feature of right traveling is to be vague about where you are traveling, for this indicates an absence of familiar but wrong ideas.

1293. Taking the familiar as the right is like praising a persistent thief because you recognize his methods in stealing your money.

1294. Encourage your striving toward the inner unknown.

1295. As sad as you may be over leaving the familiar but wrong world, leave it, and the sadness will vanish.

FRUSTRATION IS UNNECESSARY

1296. The day of most people consists of expecting and meeting one fearful and baffling frustration after another.

1297. Frustration is trying to tell us that we are calling nothing something.

1298. The heart of every frustration is the impossible task of believing in one's own flattering self-image.

1299. We are frustrated because we demand *our* answer over *the* answer.

1300. Nothing is more useless and frustrating than trying to make sense of life without first making sense of oneself.

1301. It is a mistake to believe that peace is present just because frustration is temporarily absent.

1302. There is no way to convince yourself that you are not frustrated, but there is a way to end frustration.

1303. These truths enable you to no longer feel blocked every way you turn.

LIGHT AND DARKNESS

1304. Light does not want to destroy our happiness, to the contrary, it wishes to destroy our pretense of happiness.

1305. One feature of darkness is that it cannot see how it suffers from itself.

1306. Light has nothing to say to raging darkness.

1307. Since darkness is egotism, it very carefully avoids the light which would end the dark egotism.

1308. A light-spreading mind sees no surrounding darkness.

1309. No matter how cunningly disguised, rudeness and contempt arise from inner darkness.

1310. To be like the light we must be in the light.

1311. Self-light brightens by noticing how many dark moods you permit to roam your mind daily.

1312. Inner darkness is cold, inner light is warm.

1313. There was once a peculiar person who complained of the shadows and yet refused to walk toward the light.

1314. Spiritual sleep attributes power to darkness when it has no power.

1315. Inner darkness is ended by leaping into it.

1316. Doubting our sincerity about wanting the light is a needful step toward the light.

1317. If you are light, there is no dark world.

1318. The last thing your habitual nature wants you to do is shine the light on it, so shine a blazing light on it.

1319. Love light.

1320. Sometimes just a right nudge from a truth or a teacher is enough to make a new light dawn.

1321. *Your* path can be illuminated by *your* light.

FREEDOM FROM TIME

1322. Time is created by the ordinary mind, and transcended by cosmic consciousness.

1323. Rise above the illusion of time and you will have tomorrow's wisdom today.

1324. Live freshly every moment by seeing that mere thoughts about a past experience do not create a present reality.

1325. Anxiety over future life is promoted through neglect of the present life.

1326. If you plan your future by your past, your future can only duplicate your past.

1327. A sad act may be present but it need not be permanent.

1328. To start the inner journey, we do not need baggage from the past, but need to drop it, such as imaginary virtues.

1329. If someone condemns your past, remember that he is condemning your *past.*

1330. Submission to the past is submission to anguish.

1331. Rightness never fears a future event, for it carries its capacity right up to the event.

EXPLANATIONS OF CRUELTY

1332. Cruel people feel a false thrill in hurting others, for they mistakenly assume that cruelty is strength.

1333. Cruelty is a good example of a human being out of control.

1334. Wrong thinking thinks that cruelty is a necessary weapon to fight supposed threats.

1335. Cruel people are scared people who know no other way to relieve their terrible tension.

1336. Cruelty develops into mechanical behavior as a result of foolish admiration of other cruel people.

1337. Awareness of the self-punishment in cruelty can help end it.

UNDERSTAND SUFFERING AND HEARTACHE

1338. Whether understood or not, the cause of all suffering is a false idea of who we are.

1339. The real self cannot feel anguish, but anguish is clutched because it seems to confirm the imaginary identity.

1340. Anguish falls away with the falling away of the imaginary self.

1341. One kind of suffering occurs when other people do not support our desperately-held illusions.

1342. A sad condition grips you only because you grip it.

1343. Egotism can never succeed in ending secret suffering, for it is the very cause of suffering.

1344. Firmly refuse to allow anguish to succeed.

1345. Despair is caused by trying to find life-answers where they do not exist, for example, in excitements.

1346. Artificial virtues cause conflict and pain.

1347. Regardless of what millions of people believe, there is no virtue in suffering.

1348. The false self feels hurt, not you.

1349. There is no need to be in despair over *anything*.

1350. Suffering used wisely leads to higher wisdom, while suffering which breeds bitterness causes more suffering.

1351. Unawareness hurts.

1352. There is no way to hurt and humiliate an awakened person, for he has no false self to get hurt.

CLIMB TO HIGHER VALUES

1353. No man searches for solid life-values until questioning his present shaky values.

1354. Review what you call valuable, then wonder whether there might be higher values unseen as yet.

1355. Only your own inner treasure has value.

1356. You will never convince a desert fox of the existence of mountain peaks.

1357. Disillusionment is trying to tell us we have wrong values.

1358. If wishing to find a higher way to travel through life you must not consult your memory.

1359. Only a willing nature can hear good news from a higher source.

1360. If you have doubts about the value of earthly success you should increase them ten times.

1361. Higher facts are true eloquence.

1362. You can understand anything above you, providing you are willing to travel above yourself.

EVENTS AND EXPERIENCES

1363. If you do not know what is happening to you, these facts will inform your mind.

1364. One way to gain real power over an unhappy condition is to question yourself instead of fighting the problem.

1365. Ask yourself, "Am I unknowingly and unnecessarily creating an unhappy condition by my own wrong thinking?"

1366. Each time you question your own wrong thinking you weaken its false power to hoax and hurt you.

1367. Events never become injuries unless we fall into wrong reactions.

1368. Human events go wrongly because they are twisted to serve human weakness and conceit.

1369. When the individual is real he cannot be attracted and trapped by artificial situations.

1370. An artificial situation is one in which sleeping people dream they are acting consciously.

1371. Tomorrow is planted today.

1372. We learn from an experience only when trying to detach our self-centered views from the experience.

1373. One good way to command some external events is to not get involved with them in the first place.

1374. A main pain of the invented self is to believe that exterior conditions should bow before its aims and desires.

1375. Be wise about the event *before* it happens.

1376. Try to see what it means to meet life consciously instead of mechanically.

1377. Any experience met by your whole mind is handled promptly, simply, smoothly, accurately.

1378. The one way to be superior to circumstances is to be superior to mechanical thinking.

1379. We can cease to be sticks of human dynamite which explode when touched by events.

1380. A beneficial experience is one causing the individual to wonder, "Maybe I am asleep after all."

1381. Until the man changes, nothing changes except his nightmares.

1382. Simply do not hide anything from yourself, then see how casually and peacefully you meet people and events.

MISUSED IMAGINATION

1383. Those who imagine they understand themselves do not want to hear anything that scares their imagination.

1384. Imagination masquerades as knowledge.

1385. A mechanical man never really knows what to do with himself because he lives from imaginary goals having imaginary rewards.

1386. The trouble with imagining we understand life is that it does us absolutely no good in a crisis.

1387. As a healthy exercise, catch yourself indulging in pointless imagination, and drop the scene.

1388. Imaginary strength is easily frightened.

1389. A sure sign of living in fantasy is to imagine that one possesses a vast quantity of unappreciated virtues.

1390. There is something beyond human imagination, and that something is what we really want.

SEE THROUGH HUMAN DISGUISES

1391. A main function of society is to deceive society, like a hungry man invited to a banquet who arrives to find no one there.

1392. What do you think people would be like if they suddenly dropped all their facial masks?

1393. There are a dozen strangers inside every person you know.

1394. What is called "social cooperation" is nothing but the mingling of personal self-interest, each hoping to come out ahead.

1395. To see what people are really like, observe their behavior when caught off-guard for a moment.

1396. Exposed deceit is always violent.

1397. There was once a talking parrot with such colorful feathers that other parrots never noticed what utter nonsense he spoke.

1398. Expecting human affairs to proceed logically or honestly simply means one has not yet seen through human masks.

1399. Accept the fact that many of your so-called friends would rejoice at your downfall.

1400. A robot dressed like a man is still a robot.

1401. Only an enlightened mind can see the insolence of a impostor *before* he gains public power.

1402. It takes superior intelligence to see through those who slyly want benefits but not corrections.

STRENGTH AND WEAKNESS

1403. Strength is determined by the number of new and right experiences one has volunteered to go through.

1404. If wishing to be exploited by other people, we need only be weak while calling ourselves strong.

1405. Weakness is simply a wrong product of wrong thinking.

1406. A feeling of helplessness can be traced back to a mental inaccuracy, and should be traced back.

1407. Neglect of development of inner strength today leaves us without new strength tomorrow.

1408. Only inner poise has real command.

1409. It is a harmful illusion that strength can be borrowed from another person or from an organization.

1410. No one grows strong by shoving his weakness onto the shoulders of someone else.

1411. Remember, you are seeking a strength that is not part of your habitual efforts.

1412. Weakness welcomes only that which resembles itself.

1413. Any pieces of truth you have which you pass along to others makes them stronger in yourself.

1414. Essence never bows down before the domineering demands of neurotic people.

1415. Borrowed strength breeds artificiality, arrogance, and finally anguish.

1416. Borrowed strength consists of wrongly thinking that mere ideas make up your identity, your individuality.

1417. A self-image of being strong is weakness, not strength, as every crisis proves.

1418. When having cosmic bravery, there is no need to think about it.

1419. A truly strong person encourages other people to take their own responsibilities.

1420. When you want to follow what is right but cannot do so, remember that your authentic nature can easily do so.

UNCONSCIOUSNESS AND UNAWARENESS

1421. Whether it is called the artificial self, the invented personality, mechanical action, evil or hypocrisy, it is all the same unconscious condition.

1422. Dazed man never knows what to do with truth, like a chimpanzee who uses a book as a toy.

1423. Those who do not ask for truth do not know they do not ask.

1424. People with betrayal in their eyes have a peculiar inability to see betrayal in the eyes of others.

1425. Unawareness of a self-harming attitude does not release us from its self-punishment.

1426. A good and simple definition of unawareness is to say that one works against himself instead of for himself.

1427. Unconscious behavior is like steering a boat straight ahead while looking backward.

1428. Self-centeredness cannot see itself, which is why it denies its existence when told about it.

1429. Ignoring the unconscious forces that terrify our life is like remaining unaware of the wild beasts in a jungle we pass through.

1430. The wild forces within can be understood and tamed by deep and persistent study of their nature.

PERSISTENCE PAYS

1431. Like a particular sentence in a book, truth is within, but requires our diligent search.

1432. Inner agony, consciously endured, destroys itself.

1433. Ordinary life becomes fascinating when you persistently absorb something higher than ordinary life.

1434. If it takes years just to see what does *not* work, the years are spent wisely.

1435. You must go through to get out.

1436. As a way to change your life, these ideas work, so submit constantly to their kindly power.

TRUE AND FALSE REWARDS

1437. Recognizing and receiving higher help is a right reward for performing preliminary tasks on your own.

1438. The real prize is never delivered by memory or by imagination, but by something above them.

1439. Some true rewards are the sensing of higher ways, ending unseen self-righteousness, thinking with your own mind.

1440. A false reward is anything contributing to delusion, while a true reward is whatever conquers delusion.

1441. Examples of false rewards are thrills to the vanity, gaining allies in wrongness, having power over people.

1442. Only ignorance craves the worthless.

1443. The reward of listening to truth when it calls us back from wandering is to no longer wander.

1444. Every effort to understand something is rewarded, even if unseen at the time.

1445. When right seeds are planted, right harvests are certain.

1446. Wrongness has its own thrilling reward, but must eventually swing over to its opposites of anxiety and depression.

1447. The one who does the inner work is the one who is rewarded by it.

1448. The harder it is to drop familiar but useless ideas, the greater the reward for succeeding.

1449. Revelation is the real reward.

1450. A real reward cannot be known in advance, which means it arrives in the absence of ordinary expectations.

1451. It should make us very happy to realize that truth never leads us astray with false rewards.

1452. The prize is overwhelmingly worth all the effort.

DELIGHTS OF THE PATH

1453. The most marvelous experience of life is to transform life according to reality, not imagination.

1454. It is proper pleasure to sense what you can do for yourself internally.

1455. A new truth often comes unexpectedly, like suddenly striking a vein of gold after mining for many days.

1456. A true pleasure is one that arises from an undivided self.

1457. Wholeness casually permits right pleasure.

1458. One small step out of mental isolation may feel scary at first, but it finally leads to a new world.

1459. Being useful to yourself is a natural pleasure.

1460. You will become increasingly skilled at adding or subtracting ideas according to their true worth.

SEE THROUGH FALSE PLEASURE

1461. Actions based on the craving for mere thrills, especially ego-thrills, waste our vital powers.

1462. The false excitement of chasing delusions blocks the right feeling of self-discovery.

1463. There is a certain false pleasure in being scolded, which badness deceitfully calls repentance.

1464. Real repentance always includes a degree of willingness to exchange egotism for reality.

1465. Despair is in love with despair.

1466. Curiously, people love the excitement of stormy seas in preference to the peaceful harbor.

1467. It is rare to find someone who prefers to end his problems instead of enjoying their agitation.

1468. It is a dreadful day in the life of a socially successful person when he begins to enjoyably imitate the arrogance of other successful people he once envied.

1469. Obedience to mechanical ways provides a strange pleasure to lazy minds.

1470. Destructive pleasure, such as revenge, always justifies itself, which means it loves to lie.

1471. Do not let yourself be carried away by society's pointless floods of impulsive enthusiasms.

1472. Clinging to harmful attitudes is a false love.

1473. False ideas about pleasure produce false ideas about right and wrong, as when a thrilling love for power justifies cruelty.

1474. One form of injurious false pleasure is to feel that one is at least a minor hero in helping a sad person.

1475. Never let exciting sensations masquerade as healing inspirations.

1476. Emotional stimulation is not the same thing as spiritual learning, though many people think so.

1477. Living in exciting imagination seems friendly, but it finally betrays us.

1478. Be available to your own interior instructions, which can be heard by not loving agitated reactions.

FACTS AND FANTASIES

1479. Basically, fantasy consists of falsely believing that one has a separate, independent, competitive identity.

1480. Facts come from heaven, opinions come from earth.

1481. When delusion talks about freedom it is like a caged parrot teaching about a liberated life in the mountains.

1482. Fantasy never wants you to investigate it, so for your own sake, investigate it all the way.

1483. The destruction of delusion is the same as genuine creativity.

1484. Fantasy is shocked and angered when seeing it cannot play its usual tricks in front of a real teacher who sees through it.

1485. Living in fantasy is its own punishment.

1486. With cosmic insight you can learn a hundred facts about another person just by observing his speech.

1487. A fact which a man does not understand does not exist for him.

1488. Fantasy is a treacherous counselor who coddles those it will eventually betray.

1489. The more acceptable a man becomes to reality the less acceptable he becomes to the masses of humanity who prefer fantasy.

1490. Learn well the basic facts of life, for the deeper the foundation the taller the building.

GIVE LIFE REAL MEANING AND PURPOSE

1491. Higher truths are for anyone who cannot find a real purpose in his or her present life.

1492. What matters is what you are doing with your own life.

1493. Think that your daily purpose is to develop a right relationship with yourself.

1494. The purpose of higher knowledge is to work for you, so make it your purpose to permit it.

1495. We need correction if we think that honors bestowed by society have real meaning.

1496. A mental fixation is not the same as having a real and steady purpose in life, but millions think so.

1497. See the purpose of self-study and it becomes a pleasure, and the purpose is self-liberty.

1498. There can be no more practical purpose in life than to be true to truth.

1499. Life's meaning is understood when we stop imposing our own meaning on it.

1500. Use your life in discovering what you need to discover, and that is all there is to it.

1501. False goals and feelings of helplessness go together.

1502. The purpose of life is not to see how many ways you can make yourself miserable.

1503. A man's day is purposeless when he spends it in unconscious nourishment of neurosis.

1504. Stupidity is a preference for suffering over learning.

1505. A chief problem with aimlessness is its strange ability to appear to have a positive purpose.

1506. You are here on earth to evolve into something higher than yourself.

1507. Have the purpose of finding yourself, and watch how all other purposes take their right place.

1508. Who you really are knows what you should really do with your life, so what a great opportunity!

FACTS ABOUT ANSWERS

1509. When having a thousand answers about life, many of them contradictory, we can be sure we do not yet have the Real Answer.

1510. It is healthy to suspect that our present answers are bluffs.

1511. When the mind is exhausted in trying to find the answer, the answer dawns.

1512. We fear to relax from a question, believing it may escape us, but the very relaxation attracts the answer.

1513. Cosmic Command has all the answers, which it gives freely to those who prefer it to human ways.

1514. Like learning to climb a majestic mountain, we can learn to view higher answers.

1515. Right answers come only from a right nature.

1516. Our part is to prepare ourselves inwardly to hear and understand higher answers.

BUILD COURAGE AND CONFIDENCE

1517. It takes courage to tell unpleasant truths to ourselves, but it dissolves the pains of untruths.

1518. False courage frantically tries to reassure itself with allies, exterior successes and man-made doctrines.

1519. Confidence must rest in knowledge, not hope.

1520. Courage to do the good and the necessary comes by a calm realization that they are good and necessary.

1521. See what it means to drop self-labels, for that draws you closer to what is truly dependable in yourself.

1522. Bravery does not consist of fighting mental pain, but in seeking to understand the pain while it persists.

1523. The courage of Cosmic Command enters those who abandon the false courage of egotism.

1524. Be factual, not philosophical.

1525. Never fear the idea that you may be deceiving yourself, rather, bravely investigate it.

1526. Fearing the inner adventure is like fearing to pick up thousands of sparkling diamonds.

HUMAN HOSTILITY TOWARD TRUTH

1527. Running away from truth in fearful hostility is one characteristic shared by billions of sleeping human beings.

1528. Facts about trueness are not acceptable to established institutions.

1529. A man lives from his artificial self to the degree that he becomes angry or evasive or bored when told about it.

1530. If you give a truthful book to an ape he will tear it apart.

1531. Someone may assure you with words that he wants to know the truth about himself, but his face warns, "Don't trifle with my illusions."

1532. When truth is attacked by obviously hostile people, do not feed their hostility by arguing in any way.

1533. Self-concern refuses to see the reality far above it, for it wrongly fears the loss of its self-idolization.

1534. Hollow minds think it is dangerous to learn something new.

1535. What an unawakened man needs from an awakened man is rarely sought by the unawakened man.

1536. Cosmic wisdom cannot explain itself to human stupidity any more than a dove can teach an ox to fly.

1537. Speak the truth to yourself, and whatever objects to that is an enemy, such as anger toward the truth.

1538. Those who want novelty in a teaching instead of the necessary medicine will soon fall away.

1539. There is no answer to a question about truth asked in a spirit of antagonism.

1540. A good way for anyone to maintain his suffering state is to respond with hostility when corrected.

1541. A wrong mind distorts rightness, not seeing what it is doing.

1542. The problem in informing people of their wrongness is that it usually falls on their resentment instead of on the wish to learn.

BANISH WORRY AND ANXIETY

1543. We must not overlook the obvious, for example, hiding anxiety will not cure it.

1544. Worry serves as a distraction from self-facing, which is why worries are carelessly created.

1545. The habit of worry simply means we prefer our worry to the effort of understanding and ending it.

1546. Worry is ended by seeing that it has no real connection with your higher nature.

1547. Anxiety is the result of dreams crowding out realities.

1548. Do not ask for relief from anxiety, but ask for insight into it, for insight is true and lasting relief.

1549. A worried mood can be dropped any time you remember that you can drop it.

1550. Anxiety must be seen as anxiety, and not called excitement or ambition or inspiration.

1551. Pretending that we are confident when we are really anxious is a good way to preserve anxiety.

1552. The chief problem in worrying about who you are—is worrying about it.

1553. The reason you need not be anxious over anything is because there is no separate self to be anxious over.

1554. When shaken by anything at all we can see that we were not living from our rightful Cosmic Command.

ELEVATE YOUR ATTENTION

1555. It is a marvelous experience just to direct the attention to something higher than our habitual thoughts.

1556. Conscious attention to wrongness enables you to no longer give it the attention that it thrives upon.

1557. Do not neglect right attention to your own life by giving wrong attention to the lives of other people.

1558. Concentrate your attention fully on the lesson of the moment.

1559. Switch the attention from self-frightening topics to self-enlightening topics.

1560. The attention of a free mind alternates naturally between inner meditation and outer tasks.

HOW TO MAKE RIGHT DECISIONS

1561. Wrong decisions tumble recklessly out of self-centeredness, while right decisions flow casually out of self-wholeness.

1562. There is great inner enrichment in making your own decisions while studying their results.

1563. There is no difference in making a decision against truth and making a decision against oneself.

1564. We walk the path we choose, but can always change our choice.

1565. By teaching conscious and prompt action, Cosmic Command erases the pain of indecision.

1566. We are indecisive and fickle because we do not as yet know what is truly good for us.

1567. Your natural self makes right decisions.

1568. When making a choice based in unconscious vanity we must then pay the high price for that choice.

1569. We learn to make right decisions by consciously bearing the consequences of our wrong decisions.

1570. A whole mind makes choices when shopping or when dressing, but never needs to choose ways to be happy.

1571. When asleep, we cannot make right choices, and when awake, we cannot make wrong choices.

1572. All decisions should be based on what is true for you, not on what is desired by you.

HELPFUL FACTS ABOUT TRUTH

1573. A pearl of truth can be recognized and valued only by those having at least a bit of truth within.

1574. No one seeks the truth fully while still concealing his inner discomfort with shallow exterior comfort.

1575. Truth is what is left when falsehood is banished.

1576. The best way to block rescuing truth is to want it to be what we want it to be.

1577. Truth is what *it* is, and when getting this fact through our heads we obtain truth at last.

1578. Truth responds to courteous requests, never to insolent demands.

1579. The only thing that separates you from truth is the thought that you are separate from truth.

1580. No one is forced to accept truth, but he must then accept the alternative of living with his hidden terrors.

1581. When a wolf can recognize Mars, an untruthful mind can recognize truth.

1582. Truth itself cannot cause pain, for pain occurs only when truth smashes against our resisting falseness.

1583. Those who reject truth think that truth-seekers have no sense, while it is the rejecters themselves who have no sense.

1584. The more a truth hurts, the more we need it.

1585. Falsehood is made up of a thousand battling opinions, while truth consists of one whole fact.

1586. A truth originating outside us rings the bell of comprehension only when striking truth inside us.

1587. Truth never speaks to arrogance.

1588. One painful compulsion of an earthly mind is to try to drag spiritual truths down to its own confused level.

1589. Truth is just waiting for us to stop talking.

1590. Anyone dominated by confusion toward truth may finally find truth, but anyone dominated by hatred toward truth cannot find it.

1591. The moment we start fighting the truth we stop learning the truth.

1592. Truth is neither a man's opinion nor its opposite opinion, but a cosmic position above all opinions.

SELF-RESPONSIBILITY IS POWER

1593. Self-responsibility is often wrongly seen as a burden, when it should rightly be seen as an opportunity.

1594. Using a borrowed spiritual key is risky, for you only have the other man's word that it will open the door.

1595. Nothing can supply higher life but personal effort, though deceivers will tell you otherwise.

1596. Attribute your troubles to your misunderstanding and you have made a right move.

1597. Live by, "I do not know but I will find out."

1598. The more a man has abandoned self-responsibility the more he will preach social responsibility.

1599. Cosmic Command is acquired by taking new and small responsibilities each day for inner development.

1600. Continued confusion indicates a lack of self-responsibility in some way.

1601. Others may have hurt us in the past, but now we are responsible for tossing out the damage.

1602. Our part is to see the need for something totally new, for that enables reality to supply it.

IGNORANCE AND STUPIDITY

1603. Society is like a chorus of defective singers, each trying to hide his faultiness by singing with others.

1604. Stupidity dreams it is intelligence.

1605. The owner of absurd ideas is the one who has to live with them.

1606. Small minds are delighted with each other.

1607. The indignant man is simply someone who gets the same kind of treatment he gives unconsciously.

1608. Ignorance is always unhappy.

1609. Never speak to stupidity as if it is intelligence.

1610. Inward sleep is always unconscious, which means the sleeper will always deny being asleep.

1611. Stupidity is highly popular with the stupid.

1612. Those who require the most patience in dealing with them are the least likely to realize it.

1613. Evil is tormented by its own stupidity.

1614. Those who refuse to sacrifice error will gladly sacrifice you.

HIGHER LOVE

1615. Truth is very much concerned that everything is all right with you.

1616. Love is the very nature of Cosmic Command.

1617. We are told we are living wrongly only as a kindly guide toward living rightly.

1618. When truth does not allow us to behave in our usual ways it is expressing its compassion.

1619. Something wiser than you is always ready to help you.

1620. Truth penetrates us wherever it finds an opening, like a shaft of sunlight in a dark forest.

HOW TO UNDERSTAND PEOPLE

1621. Collect helpful facts about human nature, for example, see that a cold-mannered person is also scared.

1622. The problems anyone has with others will be equal to the problems he has with himself.

1623. Weakness pounces on weakness with great glee.

1624. Remember that a defeated and pathetic person always has dangerous and concealed hostility in him.

1625. No person and no organization has real power to mislead you.

1626. A man exploits others to the degree he has already exploited himself.

1627. Arrogance is always about ready to cry.

1628. Anyone unable to do truly good things for you will not appreciate truly good things you do for him.

1629. The human masses try to destroy human individuality.

1630. Self-righteousness loves to pounce on an evil which by sheer accident is not its particular evil.

1631. Human beings are most generous with virtues they do not have.

1632. A chief rabbit told his young followers, "Beware of a fox that invites you to his home for a carrot dinner."

1633. Insolence is weakness masquerading as courage.

1634. Observe how people slyly suggest their importance, as when complaining over the many phone calls they receive.

1635. Mr. A, the new and trusted ally of Mr. B against Mr. C, is already thinking of becoming the new and trusted ally of Mr. C against Mr. B.

1636. Human follies are often very polite and well-dressed.

1637. When someone behaves badly toward you he tends to avoid you, for you remind him of his weakness.

1638. Power over others breeds contempt for them.

1639. It is a world of pathetic people going through the agonizing motions of trying to appear real.

1640. Our aim is to understand people, not fear or criticize them.

THINK TOWARD YOURSELF BENEFICIALLY

1641. Useless initiative is aroused by craving to prove oneself, while profitable initiative is awakened by wanting to find oneself.

1642. Dropping wrongness magically reveals rightness.

1643. Bitterness fades by seeing that nothing really cheats us but our own misunderstanding of self and life.

1644. Self-condemnation is an unnecessary weight.

1645. A typical mistake is to feel that others have more happiness or excitement than we do.

1646. Temptation is a testing by hostile feelings to see whether you will give them power, which you must not do.

1647. Drop false values by seeing they do not work for you, which takes immense courage and honesty.

1648. Make sense to yourself.

1649. We should keep in good with rightness because it makes no sense to do anything else.

1650. Give needed thought to your outer future, but give your whole life to your inner future.

FALSE TEACHINGS

1651. A false teaching is any teaching which pretends to erase egotism while actually increasing it.

1652. The confused teach the confused, and both walk away wondering what it was all about.

1653. A false teacher and his false followers are slaves of each other.

1654. Any doctrine needing allies is useless, and not your own.

1655. Because a false teaching has no conscience, it uses every deceitful device for keeping its followers dependent.

1656. Man-made doctrines about good and evil obstruct true good.

1657. False teachers claim they wish to help the world, when in fact they are trying desperately to convince themselves.

1658. Spreading confusion is a trick of unclear minds pretending to be clear.

1659. One aim of a false teaching is to help someone believe that all is right when it is really all wrong.

1660. Any teaching which avoids self-facing is untrue.

1661. Falsehood posing as truth will compromise with deceit, while real truth will have nothing to do with deceit.

1662. A main task of falsehood is to hate and attack anyone who might expose it.

1663. A man who owned a tree bearing sour apples went around lecturing on the dangers of eating sweet apples.

1664. False teachers succeed because of false followers.

1665. A false teaching will use every damaging device possible to subtly suggest you are not responsible for yourself.

1666. A true teaching will never let you evade the fact that you are responsible for yourself.

HUMAN LUNACY

1667. It is not the possession of a conscience but the lack of an opportunity that prevents most human crime.

1668. Lunacy thinks sanity is lunacy.

1669. A chief aim of organizations devoted to peace is to destroy each other.

1670. Merely blocking human lunacy is pointless, for it will just break out in another place.

1671. Every insane human activity is called sane by anyone getting a false identity from it.

1672. A lunatic calls his lunacy love.

1673. Human lunacy is never more hideous than when it demands an explanation from reality.

1674. Hallucination is often mistaken for revelation.

LEARN ABOUT COSMIC LAWS

1675. To understand how things work on a higher level we must actually become that higher level.

1676. For good or bad, we attract what our actual nature requests.

1677. Low causes, low effects.

1678. Right firmness with yourself will naturally extend itself into right firmness with others.

1679. Fantasies fear facts, while facts ignore fantasies.

1680. What we do for or against the truth is what we do for or against ourselves.

1681. No one can be unhappy with himself and still be happy with others.

1682. A wish for truth attracts rescuing facts, while a demand for thrills attracts punishing delusions.

1683. Your world is exactly what you are.

1684. Truth never gives one human being personal and material advantages over another person.

1685. We hear only those truths we are ready to hear.

1686. You can prophesy correctly that a troubled mind will run into trouble wherever it goes.

1687. The one who commits a mental error is the one who must pay for it.

1688. When free of a negativity in your mind you are also free of it in your life.

1689. We understand cosmic laws by placing ourselves under them.

DISSOLVE YOUR TROUBLES

1690. Troubles, rightly met and understood, are the one great chance you have for ending troubles.

1691. Study and ponder what it means to meet troubles consciously, instead of wrongly attributing power to them.

1692. We wrongly credit power to troubles only when we are inwardly asleep while dreaming we are awake.

1693. To solve what bothers you, first see what bothers you, which means self-exploration.

1694. Each time you see a problem, also see the unenlightened mind as the cause of the problem.

1695. Go beyond the self that thinks in terms of troubles.

1696. The worst thing you can bring into troubles you are trying to end is despair over ending them.

1697. Real understanding breaks through as we cease to block it with habitual and impulsive thought.

1698. A sensible task when having troubles is to honestly see how we unconsciously attracted them.

1699. Just as it is the nature of the sun to shine, it is the nature of Cosmic Command to shine its solutions on human problems.

THE POWER OF TRUTH

1700. Truth can be simply defined as a calm and self-complete state of knowing, needing neither allies nor defense.

1701. By pleasing truth you please yourself.

1702. Only the entrance of new and right ideas can reveal the need to reject old and wrong ideas.

1703. Truth alone can inform what is right for you because it alone knows what is right for you.

1704. When we step off the path, truth waits patiently for us to see our mistake and return.

1705. Truth is independent of anxiety.

1706. Truth can be a blocking wall or an open highway, depending upon a person's level of inner development.

1707. It is indeed the truth that makes us free, but truth is not what we *call* truth.

1708. When the desire for truth triumphs, all other desires are understood and commanded.

1709. A study of the false reveals the true.

1710. Truth is the only force on earth that will not betray you after asking for your obedience.

1711. Opening ourselves to our own inner light reveals the difference between truths and trifles.

1712. Light is not intimidated by darkness, nor does right feel pressured by wrong.

1713. A fresh insight comes as an unexpected delight, like sighting a single flower in the desert.

1714. The power of truth becomes self-evident when we stop assuming we know what we are doing with our lives.

1715. Truth is universal medicine.

1716. When truth is profoundly recognized, obedience to it is a natural pleasure.

1717. Only God, Truth, Reality, can love us without approving of our present behavior.

THE NECESSARY AND THE UNNECESSARY

1718. An individual begins the change the moment he or she sees truth as a personal necessity.

1719. It is neither right nor necessary to involve yourself emotionally with society's sickness.

1720. When thinking painfully, think, "It is not necessary to think this way."

1721. Truth, being power, does not believe in the necessity of human weakness.

1722. One absolute necessity is to give up all excuses for avoiding self-examination.

1723. Seek self-wholeness simply because it is necessary.

RELIEF AND RELEASE

1724. There is a feeling of relief even in deciding to try to do what is right with your life.

1725. Relief and release occur when seeing the uselessness of trying to find the illusory self.

1726. Do not defend yourself enough times and you will happily see there is no one to anxiously defend.

1727. It is not necessary to fight it because it is possible to understand it.

1728. Do not assist an unpleasant person, for example, do not tensely defend yourself against an angry accuser.

1729. What a relief to no longer need to give advice to others!

1730. Feel self-release by deciding to live only and wholly from the rules of your own truly right nature.

1731. When we are really real we are under no pain or pressure to convince ourselves of it.

1732. There is no need to try to force other people to agree with you.

1733. What a great relief to no longer expect anything from confused people but confused behavior.

1734. A relaxed mind resembles an open gate which allows the endless flow of the good and the healthy.

1735. As hard as it seems, journey on, for though you may not yet know it can be done, it can be done.

MAKE DAILY PROGRESS

1736. Self-rescue comes closer each time we voluntarily come face to face with our own ignorance.

1737. Look honestly at your life as it now unfolds, then refuse to believe it must continue this way.

1738. Forget long and confusing leaps forward, instead, take small steps forward that your essence knows is right.

1739. Go fast and far by seeing what it means to start life anew, not every day or hour, but every second.

1740. Think each day about self-change instead of circumstance-change.

1741. Whatever you can do at a particular stage in your journey is the right thing to do at that stage.

1742. Be intense but not strained toward inner discovery.

1743. Inner progress ends the enmity between thoughts and feelings and turns them into allies for self-awakening.

1744. Anything that destroys the need to appear right before other people is a good thing.

1745. Spiritual progress changes your mind as to what is good and bad for your life.

1746. Use everything for inner advancement.

1747. Inner progress is slow or swift, according to the amount of humiliation to the vanity we are willing to take.

1748. Notice anything that runs away with your self-command, and refuse to cooperate with it.

1749. Accept endless inner progress for yourself and that will be your happy activity.

TRIUMPH OVER NERVOUSNESS

1750. Timidity toward the exterior world is caused by inadequate knowledge of the interior world.

1751. Hope is wobbly, while insight is firm.

1752. Restlessness cannot be seen and conquered until we stop giving it false titles, such as "constructive action."

1753. When inwardly right we remain relaxed over the results of that rightness.

1754. Nervousness can be a helpful message that our action has a wrong motive.

1755. A nervous life indicates we are unknowingly living from wrong imagination masquerading as rightness.

1756. The artificial self can never be anything but insecure.

1757. The world works the way it works, not the way we believe it works, and self-harmonious people know this.

1758. To live with self-command you need only connect yourself with natural Cosmic Command.

1759. Remain relaxed, for nothing really prevents it.

UNDERSTAND THESE TEACHINGS

1760. We must learn how to learn, for instance, we must see how our capacities are drained by chronic complaint.

1761. When anyone says he is thinking of you he is really thinking of himself in relation to you.

1762. In higher living there is no personal giver or receiver, but only a natural and alternating flow of giving and receiving.

1763. We never see another person clearly when seeing him through our demands and desires and hopes.

1764. Never agree to the terms of a wrong person.

1765. Every downstream drifter is under the dreary delusion that he is personally paddling his canoe to secure shore.

1766. Truths which cannot appear to ordinary logic present themselves to anyone who dares to drop his ordinary logic.

1767. If you work long enough without pay you will finally be paid, and it happens when you no longer imagine the nature of the payment.

1768. As the cup must precede the drink, spiritual facts must precede enlightenment, but they are not enlightenment itself.

1769. It is those who do not know who angrily argue.

1770. Your nature, high or low, is the reason you do everything you do, and there is no other reason.

1771. What life is all about is not what most people think it is, for life is all about inner awakening, which few people think about.

1772. Obeying orders from a true teacher is a necessary requirement for finally taking orders from our true nature.

1773. The height of the reward is in proportion to the height of the obstacle you hurdle.

OVERCOME OBSTACLES

1774. At the start, obstacles to real self-change are not seen as obstacles, but are wrongly called right beliefs or solid facts.

1775. One true thought can eliminate a thousand false assumptions and their damage.

1776. The more obstacles the greater the opportunity to grow strong by climbing over them.

1777. One obstacle which many must overcome is the belief that spiritual items are good as outer ornaments only.

1778. Even your yearning for the light is a kind of strength which overcomes many obstacles.

1779. Memorize the sentence, "Ordinary thinking obstructs higher understanding."

1780. One way to lower resistance to rescuing facts is to honestly observe our resistance.

1781. Like an airplane above the clouds, higher is clearer.

SURPRISING AND HELPFUL FACTS

1782. The real problem is not sex or loneliness or failure or helplessness, but wrong thinking.

1783. Inner power enables you to be nicely alone when with others.

1784. Some people know so much they disqualify themselves from knowing truth.

1785. We lose enemies when no longer having a false need for them.

1786. Your deliberate walk into your own inner darkness enables your own cosmic sun to rise.

1787. Life works in a different way than we imagine.

1788. Because a bad idea is familiar we believe it has value, and so we let it go with unnecessary sadness.

1789. The jolt we feel is truth refusing to agree with falsehood.

1790. People fail to realize that they actually fear the very truth that could make them free.

1791. We must replace hypocritical human moralities with cosmic conscience.

1792. No one is betrayed by other people without first betraying himself.

1793. Breaking away from dependence upon wrong methods produces an internal crisis, but a right and healthy crisis.

INNER AND OUTER

1794. We wrongly look outward to get something when we should look inward to understand something.

1795. Whether knowing it or not, we make our personal conditions whatever they are.

1796. Interior confusion must express itself in exterior disorder, just as a trembling tree casts a shaky shadow.

1797. You command an exterior crisis by not being part of it internally.

1798. Mental chattering ruins exterior poise.

1799. An awakened person knows how to be fully active in society while remaining safely inconspicuous.

1800. Cosmic insight alone into conditions can uplift them.

1801. Do not imagine that the exterior world strains you, but know that the strain you feel is *your* strain.

1802. It is impossible to be inwardly foggy and also be outwardly clear.

1803. Understand the inner and we understand the outer.

1804. A person goes along with the dizzy crowd because he first goes along with his own dizzy thoughts.

1805. Few people want inner valor because it brings no public applause.

1806. Correct behavior toward oneself guarantees correct behavior toward others.

1807. Inner rightness equals outer independence.

1808. Everyone who treats himself harshly wrongly attributes the harshness to someone or something outside himself.

1809. The exterior world resembles the interior world.

1810. If you wish to know why you live as you live it is because you are what you are.

1811. It is what you see internally that changes your life.

BE YOUR OWN HEALER

1812. An individual turns toward health when deeply seeing no real profit in remaining as he is.

1813. Do healthy things for yourself and do not waste energy on those who prefer unhealth.

1814. Our preference for a familiar belief stops us from rising above it to the healing fact.

1815. Painful desire exists inside the individual, not in the object of desire, so healing must also occur within.

1816. Healing enters us to the degree that we enter healing.

1817. When victimized by people we must wisely turn it toward healing insight, not toward self-centered bitterness.

1818. Self-healing occurs as we place healthy facts before thrilling fantasies.

1819. Toss out the useless medicine *first*, after which the healing medicine becomes available.

1820. Let fictions fade fast.

1821. Repeat healthy instructions to yourself, and you will see an inner obedience.

1822. Living the truth is the same as having healing power.

1823. Basically, inner health consists of seeing that one is a noncompetitive part of the Cosmic Whole.

REMOVE YOUR BURDENS

1824. Unconscious self-centeredness is a burden to its owner and to everyone else it meets.

1825. The usual kind of life on earth is heavy, and only the higher way can cure the heaviness.

1826. The old masquerades as the new, but still burdens us with the same old feelings.

1827. If we decide to leave our burdensome ways, it is about time.

1828. It is a terrible burden to try to force the wrong to appear as the right.

1829. Realize that the burden you bear about a person or event is the burden of incorrect thought toward it.

BE A GOOD STUDENT

1830. It is hard for people to grasp the plain fact that they will comprehend more by studying more.

1831. The student's light is growing when he feels less and less threatened by the teacher's lessons.

1832. Be especially eager to listen when told of your weaknesses.

1833. A real student is one who realizes, even dimly, that he cannot have both his way and the new way.

1834. Regardless of how much you learn, always be a student.

1835. Do not expect an awakened teacher to conform to your ideas of what he should be like and look like.

1836. Read receptively.

1837. Learn how to work correctly on yourself, for example, refuse to fear sarcastic people.

1838. It is right to feel you can know more than you now know.

1839. You will always do right in permitting yourself to be overwhelmed by truthful principles.

METHODS FOR COSMIC COMMAND

1840. Ponder the idea of having a clear mind, then collect facts which contribute to this happy kind of mind.

1841. If others insist upon dominating a conversation, let them, while you study their compulsive talking and your own impatience.

1842. As an experiment, instead of trying to make things happen, just let things happen.

1843. Ponder the meaning of thinking outside of yourself.

1844. Study your daily ways scientifically, neither praising nor criticizing what you see.

1845. Try to understand what you are doing *at the precise moment of doing it.*

1846. Upon arising in the morning, renew your aim to meet daily events freely and consciously, not with mechanical reactions.

1847. Try to see the self-punishment in having a negative nature.

1848. There is great wisdom in simply not interfering where we should not interfere, so find your own examples of this.

1849. See how long you can stay with and ponder right ideas.

1850. A mind rising in wisdom asks constantly, "Is this really good or really harmful for me?"

1851. Desire to go against every inward part that has no desire to awaken.

1852. It is valuable practice to write down and restate an impressive truth in your own words.

1853. Harmful self-righteousness can be cancelled by seeing our own weakness and that of others at the same time.

1854. Give up one wrong idea today.

1855. As an exercise, notice whether your activity at a particular time is mainly mental, emotional or physical.

1856. See the difference between doing what you always do and doing what is right for your internal nature.

1857. Learn to think in short and clear sentences.

1858. Search very carefully and you will never find anything wrong with an admission of being wrong.

1859. You help yourself remember these truths by becoming aware of how easily you forget them.

THE WISDOM OF SELF-EXPLORATION

1860. Self-exploration is not a popular topic to vanity.

1861. When exploring the inner world, be willing to be surprised, baffled, upset, or anything else helpful and necessary.

1862. Think that a fault may be unseen instead of unlikely.

1863. When first working inwardly it will seem as if there are many strangers inside you, which is a normal stage that will eventually go away, leaving you at ease with yourself.

1864. It takes real intelligence to explore beyond our first impulsive reaction to anything.

1865. Examine errors.

1866. The exploration is inward, the discovery is inward.

1867. Behavior toward another person that causes self-disturbance is behavior needing self-study.

1868. To see, first see that you do not see.

1869. Pause in your reading of this book to be aware of whatever thoughts and feelings you may be experiencing right now.

THE NET OF DELUSION

1870. When all are deluded they easily come to the solemn conclusion that all are sane.

1871. The delusion of having wisdom creates the dangerous delusion of having power, leading to disaster.

1872. Delusion is very attractive, but only to the deluded.

1873. Delusion delivers punishment, but snares men by calling the punishment a reward, as when delivering thrills to vanity.

1874. When delusion accidentally approaches truth, it falls away just as accidentally, for it cannot recognize truth.

1875. Delusion delivers dread.

1876. Delusion does nothing for us but deceive us into thinking it can do something for us.

1877. See a delusion as a delusion by seeing its discomfort.

CONQUER GLOOM AND DEPRESSION

1878. A man is gloomy according to the number of things he knows about himself that he would rather not tell himself about.

1879. It is a sign of psychic sleep to suffer from ourselves without knowing why.

1880. Dread can end because its cause of wrong thinking can end.

1881. Far better than learning how to dry tears is to learn how to not cry in the first place.

1882. Take away tears and you make a lot of people sad, for tears are one of their great moments in glorious self-dramatization.

1883. Dejection is abdication of life.

1884. Discouragement is simply a wrong internal movement caused by wrong beliefs about ourselves.

1885. One good reason for abandoning falsehood is that it is always so gloomy.

1886. No law compels you to be depressed by depressed people.

1887. Mere belief is depressing, for believing that one has the answers does not satisfy the need for actually possessing answers.

1888. Self-delusion cannot be separated from self-dejection.

1889. Depression is based on the false belief that you have a separate self which must be affirmed by others.

1890. Gloom is simply one of the dozens of directions which unawareness can take.

1891. Cosmic Command cannot be depressed because it has no artificial interests to be depressed about.

SELF-UNITY

1892. A man believes he is a single, consistent person, when in fact he is dozens of different and contradictory selves.

1893. Self-unity is the result of dissolving the many conflicting selves within, to live from single and whole essence.

1894. When craving something one minute and rejecting it the next we reveal lack of self-unity.

1895. End harmful desires by desiring self-unity.

1896. The nice thing about self-unity is that one can take care of himself in all situations, including the unexpected.

1897. Union with God, Truth, Reality, is the same as union with oneself.

ATTAIN HIGHER SUCCESS

1898. A wish for something higher acts as springtime to the sleeping seed of consciousness.

1899. We can either have our own way, and lose, or lose our own way, and win.

1900. Wherever you are, you can climb much higher.

1901. Words have limited ability to describe the higher world, which is why we must stride beyond the description to the experience.

1902. We have wings for soaring, but neglect their use.

1903. All advancement toward a higher mind is made with conscious fear and trembling.

1904. To win something higher, risk all you think you have won.

1905. Elevate essence.

1906. Stick consciously with a difficulty, and it will of itself tell you how to rise above it.

1907. Never linger on an upward step, but ascend to the next.

1908. Refusal of the lower is acceptance of the higher.

1909. Reading these facts builds the rocket, while working with them makes the rocket fly.

FREEDOM FROM SELF-CONFLICT

1910. We need the honesty to admit many inner conflicts, for conflicts are sure signs of an unconscious life.

1911. Man's problem can be described simply as a painful inability to either stop or go.

1912. Man is trapped in the contradiction of wanting his egotism while wishing to avoid its painful results.

1913. We might as well stop trying to convince ourselves that our worthless involvements are important.

1914. First live in heaven, after which you will live easily on earth, which means you will not be in conflict when deciding between tea or milk for lunch.

1915. There are hundreds of ways to refuse true spiritual education, and every one of them causes inner conflict.

1916. False ideas invent false demands which cause frustration.

1917. Self-conflict occurs when feelings do not agree with thoughts, and when outcomes do not match desires.

1918. Wanting both reality and self-will is like wanting spring and winter to occur at the same time.

1919. Conflict is not a mystery to be complained about, but a condition to be solved.

BREAK THE SELF-TRAP

1920. Our prison is our hardened misunderstanding, and our liberty is its melting.

1921. To break out into a new world it is first necessary to break out of your present identity.

1922. No interior nor exterior false power can chain you against your wish.

154

1923. A free mind is one that failed so dismally in living up to its flattering self-images that it gave them up entirely.

1924. You are now learning what it means to have nothing to do with your own nagging thoughts.

1925. Challenge chains.

1926. There is a way to view life without painful self-reference, which is the way of Cosmic Command.

1927. Fighting the scary situation is the same as fighting yourself.

1928. Your unconscious acceptance of the limits of your existence is what limits your existence.

1929. Deliberately expose wrong attitudes which do not want to be exposed.

1930. True self-rescue consists of seeing there is no self to rescue.

1931. The habitual self cannot go to truth, but when the self fades through insight, truth is there.

1932. Give yourself power to no longer tear yourself apart.

1933. Replace self-accusation and self-condemnation with self-study and self-awareness.

1934. Just to sense how we are trapped by our own fixed beliefs and habits begins to break the trap.

1935. Your storm alone keeps out your sun.

1936. Be truly conscious and you will be right, but be unconscious while dreaming you are awake and you will be wrong.

1937. The painful trap is our self-centered stubbornness.

1938. Release your true nature to do what it wants, and you will not fear the wild demands of the old nature.

1939. You can find the way out by being aware of your fear of the facts, then letting acquired insight explain the falsity of the fear.

HOW TO BE YOURSELF

1940. The only person you must be like is yourself.

1941. Ponder the idea of not allowing people to steal your mind.

1942. Sin can be rightly defined as anything that separates us from our real nature.

1943. You are rightly trying to give yourself yourself.

1944. What is truly your own is also universal.

1945. A confused man heard, "Instead of trying to convince others that you are someone you are not, why not simply become real?"

1946. Try to hear the voice that calls you back to yourself.

1947. Stop being who you now assume you are.

1948. Anything living solely from its own nature lives at ease, whether a sycamore, a bluebird, or a human being.

1949. Liberate life.

HOW TO BRIGHTEN CONDITIONS

1950. Human methods make the world what it is, and only celestial methods can change it.

1951. Bring even a small portion of truth into an everyday condition, and it will work at once to brighten that condition.

1952. There is no real need to be involved in a troublesome involvement, so walk quietly out of it.

1953. We unconsciously ask for people and events which resemble our own nature, so to uplift things, we must change our nature.

1954. Cosmic alertness will prevent you from absorbing the negative atmosphere in a social gathering.

1955. Stop trying to conquer the world and you will conquer it.

1956. A new and practical response to a troublesome event is mental and verbal silence, for it allows you to *see*.

1957. An incentive for enriching the inner is the realization that the inner will reproduce its nature outwardly.

INSIGHTS INTO ENEMIES

1958. If someone treats you with contempt, it will not hurt if it falls on your understanding authentic nature.

1959. Only a cosmically mature mind can refuse to feel pleasure at the downfall of an enemy.

1960. Do not reward an accuser by reacting in a way that thrills his false sense of power to disturb you.

1961. The more enemies within, the more enemies without.

1962. Think without anger toward demanding people, "Who said I must behave according to your demands?"

1963. With Cosmic Command you can see hostility in someone and yet not fear him.

1964. Inner division creates the dreadful delusion that it is you against the entire universe!

1965. A man's enemies consist of nothing but his own unconscious enmity.

1966. An unfree man creates an imaginary enemy which he calls real in order to also imagine himself as real and separate and an opposite of the enemy.

1967. Awareness is your friend who protects you from the enemy of unawareness in others.

SEEK SIMPLICITY

1968. The topic of *simplicity* baffles a complicated mind.

1969. An ignorant mind loves to hide its ignorance with involvement in complicated and contradictory ideas.

1970. Complexity is its own painful prison.

1971. Life-simplification arrives by bravely dropping all self-labels, both good and bad self-labels.

1972. Truth itself is simple, but complex minds distort it.

1973. Seek simplicity.

HAVE AFFECTION FOR TRUTH

1974. Prefer the true over the popular.

1975. See bewilderment as a lack of information, then love the task of acquiring the needed facts.

1976. Affection for true life is beauty.

1977. The aim of truth is to cut off all our usual escapes, so we should wisely cooperate with it.

1978. Be true to your true feelings.

1979. Affection for true knowledge increases knowledge, and then that knowledge increases affection.

1980. Be a lover of royal principles, not of odd sights and sounds.

1981. Pursue profundity.

1982. Care for truth, after which it will teach you how to care for your own life.

1983. What beautiful eagerness to try to eagerly please whatever is true!

INNER FREEDOM AND SLAVERY

1984. You have full permission to set yourself free, and nothing can deny that permission.

1985. Freedom consists in not being compelled to work against yourself.

1986. True freedom consists of doing what one really wants to do, which is not the same as doing what compulsion forces one to do.

1987. Suggestibility is slavery.

1988. Tensely hoping to come out safe in a social situation indicates enslavement to self-centered ideas.

1989. A man is enslaved by his own false doctrines.

1990. People who appear shocked at physical slavery actually rejoice in placing others in mental slavery.

1991. Freedom does not consist of doing whatever the lower impulses dictate, but of not being enslaved by lower impulses.

SELF-KNOWLEDGE IS REAL POWER

1992. Self-knowledge is power for self-transformation.

1993. Only deep awareness of one's great pain can make him see the necessity of self-knowledge.

1994. Anyone who really understands the meaning of self-injury does not do it.

1995. When you know, you will know whether or not another person knows.

1996. Acquaintance with your own mind is attained by asking constantly, "What am I thinking right now?"

1997. Self-knowledge frees you from troublesome people, like a king riding in his royal carriage who pays no attention to yapping dogs.

1998. The quality of self-insight is the quality of the life.

1999. The less one knows about oneself the more he shuns self-study, for he fears losing imaginary values.

2000. Know yourself and know where you are going.

2001. Try to see the difference between right and wrong inner instructions.

2002. One should be very grateful for all revelations as to how lost he is, for only good can come from it.

2003. Advance audaciously in self-knowledge.

2004. To see oneself as either good or bad is to not yet know oneself, for real self-knowing is above these opposite labels.

2005. Mental sleep is caused by ignorance of higher principles.

2006. Dissatisfaction with others is just the outer extension of dissatisfaction with ourselves.

2007. A man is placed on terrifying trial by no one but himself, by nothing but his own ignorance.

2008. Self-knowledge can come by noticing how we pretend to like things we really dislike.

2009. Other people understand neither themselves nor you, which means you must develop rescuing self-understanding.

2010. A right aim is to let yourself know much more about yourself than you presently know.

2011. Enjoy inner exploration.

HOW TO FEEL GOOD

2012. We feel sunny or gloomy according to our actual nature, so feel sunnier by uplifting the level of being.

2013. Learn to fall under right facts instead of wrong feelings.

2014. Emotion arising from true knowledge is constructive, while emotion aroused by wrong ideas is damaging.

2015. When we are truly sensible we can be rightly emotional.

2016. When feeling lost, turn your attention to things which are not lost, such as truthful principles.

2017. Real knowledge supplies a feeling of not being in danger.

2018. For contentment or dissatisfaction, the way we behave toward reality makes us feel what we feel.

2019. Do not seek sensational feelings.

2020. Wrong feeling separates us from people and events, while right emotion places us in harmonious relationship.

2021. Dropped error first feels painful and then feels right.

FREEDOM FROM ANGUISH

2022. Anguish can be rightly used to end anguish, for example, we can see its origin in wrong thinking.

2023. Withdraw your permission for people to hurt you.

2024. The moment the artificial self is disconnected from a sorrow, the sorrow collapses.

2025. Nothing hurts us more than the unconscious glorification of personal suffering.

2026. Anguish is not necessary because its cause— unconscious egotism—is not necessary.

2027. Do not be strangely fascinated by heartache.

2028. Understand that an unhappy mood is nothing but a bluff, then call the bluff.

2029. The only thing anguish can do is keep itself going, but your Cosmic Command can stop it.

HAUNTED HUMANS

2030. Delusion creates dozens of bewildering self-views, like a man surrounded by a hundred mirrors.

2031. Neurosis is compelled to join surrounding neurosis.

2032. The habit of defending self-wrongness keeps men and women as haunted as they are.

2033. A person who feels safe only when surrounded by people who think as he thinks is a person in danger from himself.

2034. The punisher is the punished.

2035. All anyone has to do to feel haunted is to continue to live with his present nature.

2036. Hard heart, hard life.

2037. One bad feature of self-pity is the way it encourages the illusion of having a separate self to worry over.

2038. Neurosis never knows what to do with its acquired demands.

2039. Publicly admired people are simply lost and pathetic human beings who do not know that they do not know.

RIGHT AND WRONG

2040. Anyone who lets his adopted opinions and fixed beliefs tell him what is right is wrong.

2041. Your natural essence is right every time, but will speak only in the absence of fixed beliefs.

2042. Society consists of people who decide between right and wrong who do not know the difference between right and wrong.

2043. Disorder cannot originate in rightness.

2044. We call a truth wrong because it disturbs us, when we should call it right for that very reason.

2045. Wrongness can be *felt,* and an honest admission of this feeling becomes a flash of rightness.

2046. Curiously, we fear to leave our wrongness, for that is all we have, yet leaving it attracts refreshing rightness.

2047. Be right and it is easy to do right.

2048. Society can provide an example of right behavior about as much as a duck can teach graceful walking.

2049. Right knowledge produces right judgment which produces right action which produces right days.

2050. A wrong view of another person originates in a wrong place in the viewer.

2051. Ordinary thinking may be right or wrong, but cosmic consciousness is always right.

2052. Anything lost by doing right is cause for rejoicing.

2053. We wrongly judge a thing good or bad if it conforms or fails to conform to our present opinions.

2054. One way to suffer from wrong is to call wrong right and call right wrong.

2055. An assumption can be right or be wrong, but it is wrong to insist that it is right.

2056. In human society, the right people are just as wrong as the wrong people.

2057. A nervous compulsion to prove we are right about anything is proof we are not.

2058. Nothing is easier to expose than imaginary rightness, for it turns scared and hostile when questioned.

2059. Only Cosmic Command knows the difference between right and wrong, for it has no human self-reference.

SANITY AND REALITY

2060. A higher logic exists, which can become known by everyone who wants self-unity above all else.

2061. By seeing imagination as imagination we live reality as reality.

2062. Since sanity is not sensational, it attracts little attention in society.

2063. Sanity has no doubts.

2064. Real logic is present when an idea about something and the nature of that something are identical.

2065. Truth always seems illogical at first to an illogical mind.

2066. Ignorance refuses to think about itself, while wisdom has no need to think about itself.

2067. Seek original truth, not man-made imitations.

AWAKENED HUMAN BEINGS

2068. The higher behavior of an awakened man can be seen only by those who want higher behavior for themselves.

2069. An awakened man knows every argument made by sleeping people against self-awakening, for he has heard them a thousand times.

2070. A seeker can have a real teacher or he can have his artificial nature, but he cannot have both.

2071. An awakened individual is not deceived by people who merely claim to want inner light.

2072. A teacher never tries to get through to people with whom there is no way to get through.

2073. An awakened human being knows far more about life than can be explained with words.

2074. A real teacher cannot be recognized as one unless he wishes to be.

2075. No one who departs from a true teacher realizes what he has done against himself.

2076. Everyone can see physical violence, but only an awakened man sees the enormity of mental violence.

2077. A real teacher does not try to influence human behavior, but seeks to awaken human essence which alone behaves rightly.

INSTRUCTIONS FOR TEACHERS

2078. One good program is to give a talk of about thirty minutes, followed by questions and open discussion.

2079. The teacher can read a selection from a good book, then lead the class in exploring its valuable lessons.

2080. Give variety to the class by having volunteers give short and informative talks.

2081. Remain in conscious charge of the class at all times, never permitting negative forces to take over.

2082. Control talkative members with a rule that comments should be brief and to the point.

2083. Ask students to invite friends to the class who are interested in exploring the meaning of life.

2084. Remind members that the purpose of the group is not spiritual competition but individual enlightenment.

2085. Encourage students to study and practice between meetings.

2086. An assumption that students understand less than they appear to understand is a safe assumption.

2087. Never offer any reward except truth itself.

2088. Remind the group that right intentions are of utmost importance.

2089. When teaching, remember you are dealing with scared and confused human beings who need gentle and patient guidance.

STOP BEING PUNISHED

2090. We are punished by the social system only if we mistakenly believe in it.

2091. Feel the penalty for wandering and you will want to return home.

2092. Idolizing anyone is careless abandonment of your own wisdom, which results in betrayal and sadness.

2093. We are punished *by* our wrongness, not *for* it.

2094. Feeling cheated out of worldly success is a self-punishing and unnecessary mental movement.

2095. Self-enclosure is self-punishment.

STEPS TOWARD HIGHER UNDERSTANDING

2096. Connect your pain with your misunderstanding, for until you do you will not understand nor dissolve your pain.

2097. Alertness toward the errors of others is alertness pointed in the wrong direction.

2098. Your reward or punishment for being what you are is to live with what you are.

2099. Anyone choosing fun in life over self-wholeness will not find much fun.

2100. Perhaps one person in a million can understand instead of accuse.

2101. A woman who seeks what she imagines are the advantages of a man will lose her actual benefits as a woman.

2102. Fear of anything creates the anything you fear.

2103. Man's mind in its present state is like loose cargo battering the inside of a ship caught in a storm.

2104. If you need an ally about it you are wrong about it.

2105. A man's chief love in life, for good or bad, is the one he constantly returns to after various distractions.

2106. Almost everyone makes the mistake of thinking that life-ambition is the same as life-direction.

2107. Compulsive sociality is spiritual isolation.

2108. When truth and untruth meet, truth simply watches what happens, while untruth takes mental or physical flight.

2109. An idol will always be made in our own image, and it can only supply a nervous emptiness.

2110. A chief delusion is the delusion that we have no delusion.

2111. You *are* what happens to you, for example, constant outer conflict reveals an inner nature in conflict.

2112. Giving things to people does not make them loyal to you.

2113. The harmful game we play against others is the same game we play against ourselves.

2114. You are the reason you are treated the way you are.

2115. An unawakened man spreads fear, while calling it courage, while an awakened man radiates real courage, cosmic courage.

DESPERATION IS CURABLE

2116. Desperation is simply the false product of the false self, which is cured easily and eternally by your real self.

2117. A desperate fear of not knowing not only blocks real knowing but produces a false knowing.

2118. You can drop the desperate fear of not knowing by dropping the false self which loves the desperate fear of not knowing.

2119. Angry desperation is the reaction of the artificial self to whatever threatens its shaky pretense.

2120. What you really need is the next breakthrough in self-insight.

2121. Life wants to flow by itself, but man's vanity wants to interfere with the flow, causing desperation.

2122. Stop advising heaven on how to run earth.

2123. You can replace desperation with an honest wish to discover, and you can do this any time you wish.

DO THESE GOOD THINGS FOR YOURSELF

2124. Learn to see life with cosmic light, for then there will be no doubt about anything.

2125. The moment you become aware that you can teach yourself, you already have.

2126. It is possible to not be afraid of your fear.

2127. To look rightly at a problem simply means to remember that you are not thinking rightly toward it.

2128. Consciousness that nothing else will do it enables consciousness to do it.

2129. Own yourself.

2130. The realization of how hard we work to make life hard can help break the habit.

2131. Something can be done for you when something can be done with you.

2132. It is impossible to have a right relationship with another person without first having a right relationship with oneself.

2133. The time you are hungry is the time to approach the prepared cosmic banquet.

2134. Minding our own inner business is true virtue.

2135. Sooner or later you will have to see that you cannot experience anything higher than what you are.

2136. Higher success comes our way the moment we want to be who we really are.

2137. If the weight of the world seems to be on your shoulders, remove it with this special education.

TWENTY HELPFUL REMINDERS

2138. Whatever you are going to change with the help of cosmic light, change it now.

2139. Since your present nature teaches you either self-elevating or self-depressing behavior, what are you teaching yourself?

2140. The world is empty only when we are empty.

2141. Anyone who loves his relatives more than he loves truth will be as unhappy as his relatives.

2142. The punishment for demanding your own way is to get it.

2143. Life appears against us only because we are against life without realizing it.

2144. Fear freezes intelligence.

2145. If you cannot enjoy yourself without it, you will not enjoy yourself with it.

2146. Conniving is intelligence used for harmful purposes.

2147. If you take a responsibility belonging to another you injure both yourself and the other.

2148. A person's life consists of the thoughts and feelings which govern him.

2149. A mind operating wrongly today will create a wrong tomorrow.

2150. You never have problems with what is truly right for you, but are troubled only by that which is truly wrong.

2151. The first thing a seeker must be told is that he does not want to be told very much.

2152. Truth must not be given to those who would try to twist it to satisfy egotistical needs.

2153. Have you ever noticed that you do not want to live with your own decisions?

2154. Compulsive desire has no intention of following right instruction.

2155. Having intellectual knowledge only is like owning a bookshop but not knowing what to do with it.

2156. Life treats us the same way we treat life.

2157. What another person does with his day has no connection at all with what you should be rightly doing with your day.

EXPLANATIONS OF INDEPENDENCE

2158. True independence is to be independent of our former fantasies and follies which we called virtues.

2159. Authentic independence includes independence from getting your feelings hurt.

2160. An idea about independence is not personal independence any more than an idea about bread is bread itself.

2161. Independence arrives as we see that acquired opinions are not the same as cosmic facts.

2162. Egotism calls itself independent, when it is really isolated, which explains its anxiety.

2163. We live independently in its real meaning only when living in union with cosmic wholeness.

INSPIRING PRINCIPLES

2164. Your real nature remains unconcerned with earthly results, for it knows its security does not depend upon them.

2165. When really seeing wrong as wrong it becomes enjoyable and effortless to do right.

2166. Think higher.

2167. No matter how long you have believed it, regardless of how hard you now believe it, it is *not* you against the world.

2168. Laziness loves human repetition, while energy loves cosmic originality.

2169. You have a much better thing to do with your life than to tremble over it.

2170. Though trapped by ignorance, we can escape with available wisdom.

2171. If you know it from another, you can be shaken, but if you know it from yourself, nothing can shake it.

2172. Working alone is a good exercise in independent thinking.

2173. Assumptions have their place when they are suspended judgments that are willing to let facts win over preferences.

2174. Habitual and usual thinking supplies false certainty, while absence of thought, which is consciousness, supplies solid insight.

2175. The pain of not winning, taken in the right way, can show you how to win in a new way.

ROYAL ROADS TO COSMIC RICHES

2176. Your understanding of another person's behavior toward you will show you exactly how to behave toward him.

2177. Connect a problem you have today with an idea in this book you have read today.

2178. Do what is truly right while feeling pained over it and in time the pain will go away to be replaced by a right feeling.

2179. Reality releases right relief.

2180. Never apologize for being economical with money or time or energy or anything else.

2181. You work rightly on yourself each time you remember that you forgot to work.

2182. These teachings are all about the opening of inner eyes.

2183. You love someone to the exact degree that you understand you can do nothing for them except to be an example to them of recovered sanity.

2184. Only a truth earned by yourself can be kept by yourself.

2185. A man's real cosmic maturity is revealed when he has the opportunity to pounce on another person but does not do so.

2186. Do not waste your energy by investing it in false emotional experiences, such as self-hate.

2187. Committees are confessions of individual incompetence.

2188. Each time you make yourself think for yourself you acquire eternal values.

2189. If you must risk the anger of someone in order to do what is truly right for you, then risk it constantly.

2190. Drop the belief that someone or something is trying to withhold the wisdom and power you need.

2191. The how-to-do-it consists always and only of absorbing higher understanding.

COSMIC HEARING

2192. The story of self-newness can be heard by anyone who no longer wants to hear the old fairy tales.

2193. Truth is always trying to tell us what we do not want to hear.

2194. We can hear what we want to hear or we can hear what will cure us.

2195. If afraid to hear something new, then be afraid, but be willing to hear.

2196. When we are able to bear a new noble principle, we will hear and understand it.

2197. A man can converse pointlessly with his self-centeredness, or he can listen to a lesson from his essence.

2198. When a right part of you calls for help, do not listen to a wrong part which pretends to be the helper.

2199. Let your true feelings listen to these facts.

2200. Listen carefully when your feelings try to tell you that something is fantasy, not fact.

2201. Most human beings cannot hear anything which does not promise a reward to their vanity.

2202. A seeker must acquire something he is quite sure he already possesses—the ability to listen without ego-interference.

2203. People are not only unable to hear spiritual facts, but have no idea of what it means to be unable to hear.

2204. Earthly hearing cannot comprehend celestial messages.

2205. The only person really able to listen to a teacher is one who no longer needs to shout to himself.

2206. Do not listen when wrong ideas try to explain to you why they should be retained.

2207. Listen to higher facts without the interference of mechanical mental associations.

2208. The real part of you knows whether it is hearing a truthful or a deceitful message.

2209. Cosmic Command informs us when we compromise, but we must listen to its corrective message.

END SELF-DOUBT

2210. Certainty is above both believing and doubting, and is attained by doubting our believing.

2211. End self-pretense and you end self-doubt.

2212. Self-doubt in itself can be used to end self-doubt by seeing how its agitation is based in wrong thinking.

2213. Nothing can make you sure of yourself but the self you really are.

2214. Dark minds have a compulsion to try to make you doubt the seed of truth you have found, but you can quietly refuse the evil influence.

2215. Your essence never doubts, so become your essence.

2216. Just as sand must be kept back from a desert oasis, keep doubts back by remembering these lessons.

RECEPTIVITY AND RESISTANCE

2217. The teacher offers rigorous inner training only to those who consent to it.

2218. The mind should be like an empty basket in a fruit orchard, ready to receive what is ready to be given.

2219. When the individual is ready, higher facts make an emotional impression.

2220. Real humility is an admission that God knows more than we do.

2221. No one can be called out of the human jungle who has a secret love for the jungle.

2222. Invite instruction.

2223. If some troubled people could take it, they could be given the wise and helpful advice, "Stop lying."

2224. The next time you meet a healing fact which scares you, just welcome it while being scared.

2225. Lessons are not being absorbed if we wait impatiently for the teacher to stop talking so that we can talk.

2226. Let truth succeed.

2227. If it is possible to inhale and exhale at the same time, it is also possible to listen and chatter at the same time.

2228. The opportunity to live rightly depends upon the internal reaction when one is told he is living wrongly.

ATTRACT HIGHER HELP

2229. Express even a faint wish to leave the lower and it will attract aid from the higher.

2230. Our task is to decline to cooperate with false guidance, which invites authentic help.

2231. Superb advice for changing everything is, "Watch and learn."

2232. We are rescued by a power higher than our own unconscious mechanicalness.

2233. To have something different, one can ask, but very few ask.

2234. Because our power is limited we assume that truth is as weak as we are!

2235. Wrong ideas are heavy luggage preventing flight.

2236. As we realize that human personality cannot do it for us, we permit Cosmic Command to operate for us.

AUTHENTIC ENCOURAGEMENTS

2237. No one is asked to fly at first, but is asked only to discover his cosmic wings by which he can eventually fly.

2238. No matter how long the crisis has whirled around in your mind, right explanations can calm it.

2239. When having a wrong condition you can always do something about it, as when pondering instead of worrying.

2240. What human thought cannot do, Cosmic Command is perfectly capable of doing.

2241. What baffles our artificiality is clear to our essence.

2242. No one should be discouraged, for it is possible to learn how to learn.

2243. Something can be done, but that something is totally different from our usual ways, as we eventually see.

2244. What a delight to know we can be saved from our own folly!

2245. By feeling right with your own company you will feel right in the company of others.

2246. Our forward speed increases after our first realization that truth is actually a friendly force.

2247. There is no need whatever to remain committed to a destructive course.

2248. The mansion within releases nothing but good news.

2249. Be pleased to hear that the condition made by our own darkness can be unmade by our own light.

2250. Blundering progress is still progress.

2251. The nice thing about even a bit of inner health is that it can become healthier.

2252. Years from now you will be glad you heeded these messages.

About Vernon Howard

 Vernon Howard is a unique teacher who broke through to another world. He sees through the illusion of suffering and fear and loneliness. For many years his popular books and lectures on the inner-life have all centered around the one grand topic: "There is a way out of the human problem and any earnest person can find it."

His books are widely used by doctors, psychologists, clergymen, educators and people from all walks of life. More than seven million grateful readers have experienced the power of Mr. Howard's books, including translations into a number of languages. Vernon Howard's clear insight into human nature and his practical solutions attract thousands of new readers worldwide every year.

Informal study groups of men and women use Mr. Howard's books and listen to his taped lectures. For more information, write today to:

New Life, PO Box 2230, Pine, Arizona 85544

Please send us
the names and addresses of friends
who may be interested in these teachings.

Praise for Vernon Howard